Adorn
New Jewellery

© text 2008 by Amanda Mansell
Published in 2008 by
Laurence King Publishing Ltd.

361–373 City Road
London EC1V 1LR
United Kingdom
Tel: + 44 20 7841 6900
Fax: + 44 20 7841 6910
email: enquiries@laurenceking.co.uk
www.laurenceking.co.uk

Copyright © 2008

A catalogue record for this book is
available from the British Library.

ISBN-13: 978 1 85669 574 9

Printed in China

To Mum and Dad

Title Page: Karin Seufert, *Untitled*. China,
polyurethane, Colorit, steel, 38 × 70 × 15mm.

Adorn
New Jewellery

Amanda Mansell

Contents

Introduction

As the twenty-first century marches on, the remarkably expressive art form of contemporary jewellery maintains a driving momentum of limitless, diverse enthusiasm. It is loved and enjoyed by those who create it and those who wear it and collect it. As more and more independent retail spaces open up on the high street, some owned by the jewellery designers themselves, the contagious draw of contemporary jewellery is spreading, capturing the hearts of many to whom it would not usually be accessible. As a jewellery designer and gallery owner myself, my experience allows me to tell the story of what lies behind each piece of jewellery, from inspiration to completion, enlightening this new and expanding audience.

Jewellery is for wearing. It unites with the human body, not only in its creation from mind to manufacture, but in its ultimate purpose. In adorning the body this remarkably accessible art interacts with life and our personal, everyday surroundings, transporting art from the gallery and taking it into the world for all to view.

Within the pages of this book you will find a delightfully wide-ranging and dynamic showcase of the work of new and established jewellery artists. As with all art forms, contemporary jewellery provides a platform from which to present, debate and challenge concerns or issues, such as those surrounding preciousness and value, human existence and cultural identity and memory. Lawrence Woodford creates art that reflects the beauty of nature, provoking reaction and emotion. He has consciously moved on from his formal jewellery training to investigate expression through 'worn art'. Liaung-Chung Yen's sensitively sculptural forms document the time in which she lives. She thinks of her jewellery as 'small expressions of art'. For some artists, jewellery provides a stage on which to tell a story or to have fun as depicted in the glamorous and witty work of Hannah Havana and the humorous jewellery of Felieke van der Leest. For others, jewellery is an intuitive response to form and material. The remarkably intricate and stunning work of Jacqueline Ryan takes inspiration from nature, while Georgia Wiseman creates rhythmic compositions and arrangements influenced by architecture.

One of the defining characteristics of contemporary jewellery is the integration of unconventional materials, raising questions of material value, reinvention, recycling and sustainability. Caren Hartley explores the potential of the forgotten objects to be found in a bottom drawer. By combining them with new, conventionally precious materials she 'brings them to the forefront once more, revealing their true personal value'. Similarly, Simone Nolden aims to 'reinvent found objects and reappraise unusual materials'. She elevates non-precious materials by combining them with the precious to make contemporary jewellery that challenges the traditional concept of value.

When it comes to reusing objects, the stimulus for some is to foster engagement between the wearer and maker through the expression of memory, and in turn to create fresh memories for an object once discarded. By using recycled tin cans from around the world, David Poston explores this idea, as well as drawing powerful parallels with the nature of human existence. Exploring the past and memories rooted in Dutch history, Francis Willemstijn draws intrinsic inspiration from her own cultural background, connecting the past with the present by creating new, richly referential compositions from old objects, or from materials with significant historical connections. In doing so she highlights a passion and understanding for her own cultural history and visually expresses this for others to see.

Recycling, sustainability and ethical practice are current global concerns. Laura Cave, director of Just Trade, is involved with ethical and sustainable jewellery manufacturing businesses in the shanty towns of Lima, the capital of Peru, which create some beautifully executed collections from locally available basic objects, materials and skills. Such concerns are also close to Hayley Mardon's heart. In addition to exploring these issues within her own work, she is actively engaged in projects in Kenya, working with the company MADE on collaborations that have included reforming discarded flip-flops into beads and incorporating rubber tyres into jewellery. The results of these projects, although primitive in their construction, have a unique and contemporary beauty.

At the other end of the manufacturing spectrum, continued explorations into the application of computer-aided design and manufacture (CAD CAM) have, in recent years, seen some stunning results, such as those produced by David Goodwin. This has encouraged continued debate about both the possibilities and the limitations of new technologies compared to the organic approach and traditional hand skills of artists such as Mizuko Yamada, Liz Tyler and Andrew Lamb. Describing herself as a modern-day alchemist, Angie Boothroyd painstakingly alloys her gold by hand to create a subtle palette of green, yellow and red. It can be argued that without such personal engagement a basic skill is lost, and that the touch of the hand is part of the essential experience of jewellery making. Conversely, it can also be argued that a machine working at speed allows time for further creativity or, when embraced and incorporated into the creative process, can produce outstanding masterpieces that could not be created by hand. In reality, the processes of surface finishing and additional details, such as setting stones, mean that any piece of jewellery never completely escapes the touch of the human hand.

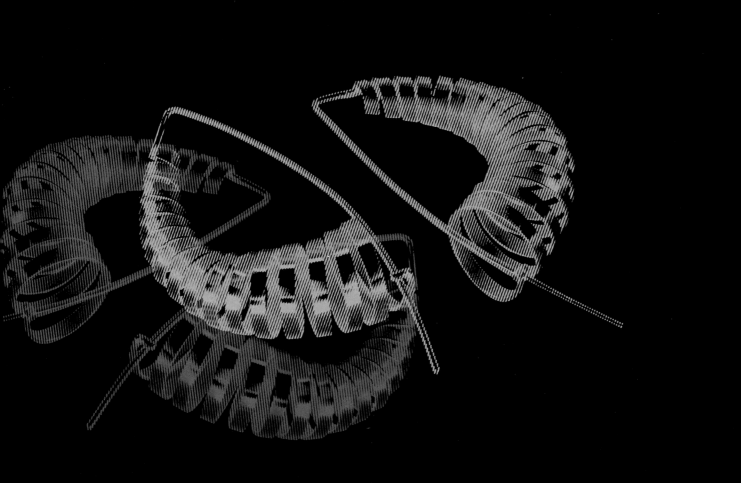

1

Earrings

THE EARS ARE VITAL
FOR OUR EVERYDAY
EXISTENCE: THEY
AID COMMUNICATION
AND PLAY A CRITICAL
ROLE IN THE PROCESS
OF BALANCE AND
MOVEMENT. SO IT
IS NOT SURPRISING
THAT WE CHOOSE TO
DRAW ATTENTION TO
THEM THROUGH
JEWELLERY, AND WISH
TO ENHANCE AND
ADORN THEM WITH
BEAUTIFUL PIECES.

Ear piercing is one of the oldest and most widespread forms of body modification. Earrings have been worn for thousands of years, with finds dating back to around 3000 BC, and have adorned the ears for reasons other than simple decoration. Ancient Mesopotamians, Greeks and Romans believed that earrings would guard against danger and prevent evil spirits entering the body, and in many cultures the size of the earrings demonstrated wealth and social status. Historical Hindu, Buddhist and Chinese sculptures depict certain important royal figures with stretched, elongated earlobes to symbolize their greatness and wisdom.

However, not all heavy earrings were worn through the lobe; they were sometimes worn in the hair or on headdresses, such as the jade ear flares worn in Central America around AD 600–1000. They were also sometimes worn around the ears and contemporary examples of this method include the beautifully sculptured ear ornaments by Apinya Oo Boonprakob, made in oxidized silver and 24ct gold, which elegantly encircle the ears, and the sculptured ice piece by Naomi Filmer.

In Western society today the wearing of earrings is increasingly common among men. In the 1970s the trend was influenced by the punk movement, while the fashion is now upheld by male music performers and professional sportsmen. However, it is evidently not just a recent craze. Paintings of William Shakespeare show him wearing an earring, and the carved images of soldiers on the palace walls in Persepolis, ancient Persia, are one of the earliest indications of men sporting such adornments. In the 1920s, earrings were also popular with sailors, who superstitiously believed that the wearing of one from a pair, with the other worn by their sweetheart, would ensure their safe return and reunion.

Contemporary earrings are still worn to signify status and beauty and are most commonly worn to enhance and frame the face. This positioning makes them highly visible and, if hanging from the lobe, will move with the wearer catching the light and coming to life. This is evident with the pink sapphires in the elegant earrings by Janis Kerman, and the additional movement allowed by this suspension in the earrings by Patricia Madeja. The versatility of the earring allows a broad range of design and scale, from the small, delicate studs by Wendy Hacker Moss, to the exaggerated length of pieces by Louise Miller, which extend beyond the ears.

Lindsey Mann, *Spinning Propeller*.
Silver, plastics, 15 × 15 × 15mm

'Each found object is a mysterious fragment of someone's past'

ABOVE: Alison Macleod, *Firenze Fairy*.
Sterling silver, cherry quartz, bra bits,
length 35mm

RIGHT: Alison Macleod, *Keepsake*.
Silver, aventurine, labradorite,
chalcedony, length 50mm

ABOVE: Angie Boothroyd, *Wildflower Bunch*. 18ct green gold, 22ct yellow gold, 22ct red gold, 18ct yellow gold, tourmalines, 10 × 30 × 10mm

LEFT: Angie Boothroyd, *Palm Cluster*. 18ct green gold, 22ct yellow gold, 22ct red gold, 18ct yellow gold, 10 × 20 × 10mm

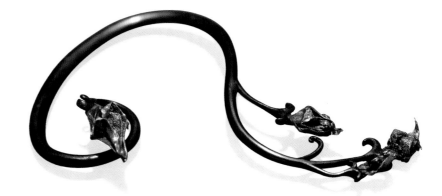

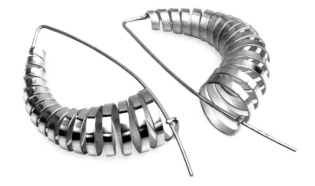

ABOVE: Daniela Dobesova, *Spiral Arch*.
Silver, 18 × 40 × 10mm

ABOVE RIGHT: Apinya Oo Boonprakob,
Ear Ornament 1. Sterling silver, 24ct gold,
65 × 5 × 15mm

RIGHT: Daniela Dobesova, *Interlocking
Spiral*. Silver, 15 × 55 × 10mm

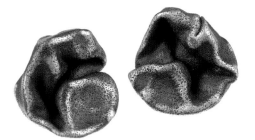

ABOVE LEFT: Rebecca Hannon, *Baroque Trefoil*. Silver, polycarbonate, 30 × 70 × 3mm

ABOVE: Sean O'Connell, *Ball*. 18ct yellow gold, stainless steel, 12 × 65 × 18mm

LEFT: Stephanie Johnson, *Crush*. Silver, 18 × 18 × 8mm

ABOVE: Lesley Strickland, *Saucer*.
Cellulose acetate, silver, diameter 25mm

RIGHT: Nutre Arayavanish, *Flourish*.
Wood sheets, gold-plated silver, oxidized
silver, freshwater pearls, 9 × 9 × 10mm

OPPOSITE: Hannah Havana,
Chandelearrings. Swarovski crystal,
gilded silver, nylon thread, electronics,
90 × 32 × 32mm

'...contradictions of fragility and great strength...'

ABOVE: Hannah Louise Lamb, *Raspberry Mismatch*. Copper, enamel, approx. 35 × 50 × 1mm

RIGHT: Marianne Anderson, *Disorder*. Oxidized silver, 18ct gold, garnet, mabe pearl, 90 × 50 × 1mm

ABOVE LEFT: Janis Kerman, *Untitled*. 18ct yellow gold, diamonds, cultured Tahitian mabe pearls, approx. 20 × 30 × 5mm

ABOVE: Ashley Heminway, *Connections*. Enamel, copper, silver, 60 × 15 × 15mm

LEFT: Shimara Carlow, *Daisy*. 18ct gold, diameter 10–20mm

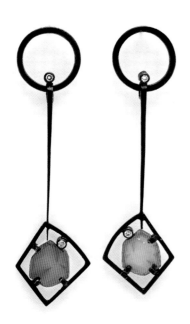

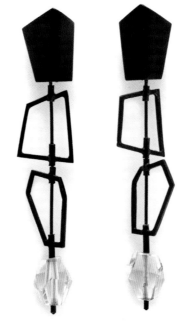

ABOVE: Daphne Krinos, *Untitled*.
Oxidized silver, tourmalines, diamonds,
55 × 12 × 5mm

CENTRE: Daphne Krinos, *Untitled*.
Oxidized silver, lemon citrines,
66 × 10 × 10mm

RIGHT: Janis Kerman, *Untitled*. 18ct
palladium white gold, pink sapphires,
amethyst and cultured Tahitian Keshi
pearls, approx. 20 × 50 × 20mm

*'Movement is an
integral component
of each piece'*

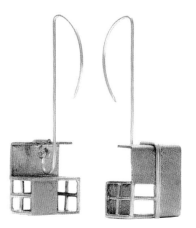

LEFT: Patricia Madeja, *Ferris Wheel*.
18ct gold, aquamarines, diamond
briolette, length 190mm

CENTRE: Janis Kerman, *Untitled*. 18ct
yellow gold, carnelian, angelskin coral,
black diamonds, approx. diameter 50mm

ABOVE: Will Evans, *Line into Form*.
18ct white gold, 18ct yellow gold,
24ct gold, 15 × 30 × 15mm

22

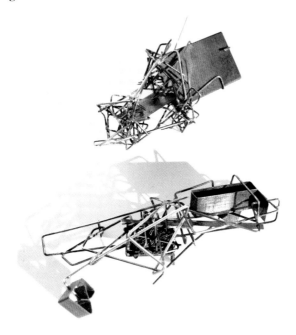

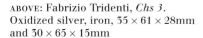

ABOVE: Fabrizio Tridenti, *Chs 3*.
Oxidized silver, iron, 35 × 61 × 28mm
and 30 × 65 × 15mm

ABOVE RIGHT: Anna Davern, *Soak* (left)
and *Possom bog* (right). Copper, brass,
sterling silver, plastic beads,
90 × 130 × 90mm

RIGHT: Anna Davern, *Mozzie Tanks*.
Brass, 18ct yellow gold, freshwater pearls,
found objects, 30 × 50 × 30mm

ABOVE LEFT: Will Evans, *Edge Beyond Form*. 18ct white gold, 18ct yellow gold, 24ct gold inlay, 48 × 118mm

ABOVE: Claude Schmitz, *Madeleine*. Fine gold, turquoise, 20 × 45 × 18mm

LEFT: Liaung-Chung Yen, 'Flourishing' series, 5. 18ct gold, diamonds, 16 × 16 × 8mm

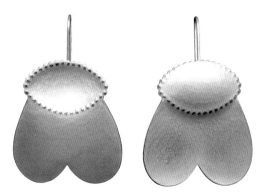

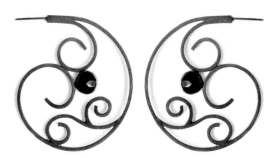

ABOVE: Birgit Laken, 'Heart Wear' series.
Silver, 45 × 40 × 5mm

ABOVE RIGHT: Marianne Anderson,
Swirl Hoop. Oxidized silver, garnets,
diameter 45mm

RIGHT: Andrew Lamb, *Untitled*. 18ct white
gold, moonstone, 10 × 8 × 8mm

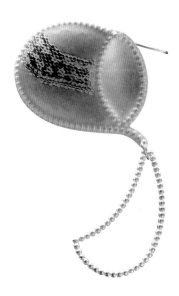

ABOVE LEFT: Wendy Hacker-Moss,
Blue Pearl. Stainless steel mesh, silver,
pearls, diameter 25mm

ABOVE: Birgit Laken, *Pouring Can*.
Silver, 80 × 40 × 3mm

LEFT: Jill Newbrook, *Untitled*. Silver, 18ct
gold, 20 × 20 × 4mm and 13 × 13 × 4mm

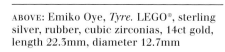

ABOVE: Emiko Oye, *Tyre*. LEGO®, sterling
silver, rubber, cubic zirconias, 14ct gold,
length 22.3mm, diameter 12.7mm

RIGHT: Tina Lilienthal, *Bone & Cherry*.
Polyester resin, silver, approx. length
5mm and 4mm

'*Taking inspiration
from old tin toys,
board games,
household gadgetry
and patchwork quilts,
Mann's work
encapsulates a sense
of nostalgia*'

Lindsey Mann, *Untitled*. Printed
anodized aluminium, silver, plastics,
95 × 20 × 10mm

'...colours, textures and patterns of fragile jellyfish, spider crabs and giant octopi...'

OPPOSITE LEFT: Louise Miller, *Very Long Earrings*. Acrylic, resin, 9ct gold, length 300mm

OPPOSITE RIGHT: Naomi Filmer, *Ice Ear-Behind*. Ice, approx. diameter 90mm

THIS PAGE: Kathy Vones, *Earconch*. Sterling silver, silicone, 350 × 500 × 350mm

ABOVE: Florence Lehmann, *Entre la raison et la passion, entre positif et ….*
Aluminium, lacquer, resin, silver, gold leaf, diameter 20mm and 40mm

RIGHT: Hongsock Lee, *Shadow.*
Silver, Keum-Bu, 50 × 30 × 10mm

ABOVE: Elaine Cox, *Untitled*. Oxidized
silver, gold leaf, 20 × 25 × 15mm

LEFT: David Goodwin, *Orb*. 18ct yellow
gold, diamonds, approx. 15 × 15 × 23mm

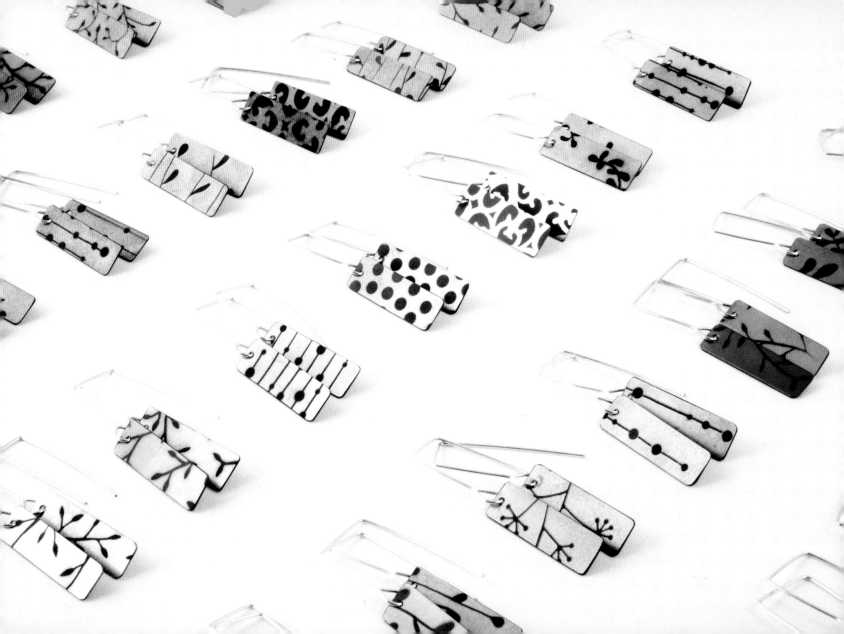

OPPOSITE: Meghan O'Rourke, *Tint*. Titanium, silver, 5 × 25 × 1mm

ABOVE LEFT: Ornella Iannuzzi, *Natural Drops*. Gold-plated silver, beetle wings, 15 × 70 × 5mm

ABOVE: Sheridan Kennedy, *Mandibulae*. Silver, antique coral, 20 × 60 × 10mm

LEFT: Louise Miller, *Paper Precious*. Paper, resin, oxidized silver, 17 × 50 × 4mm

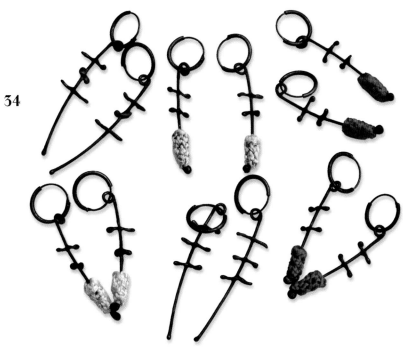

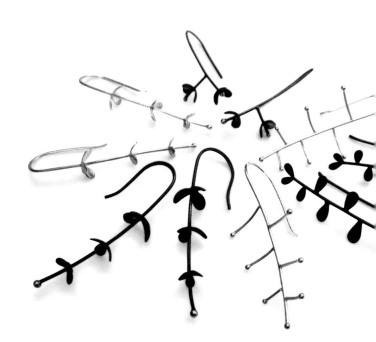

ABOVE: Joanne Haywood, *Cluster*.
Oxidized silver, textiles, 10 × 40 × 1mm

RIGHT: Laura Baxter, *Euphorbia, Sophora,
Fern, Flower*. Oxidized silver and 18ct
yellow gold, length 35mm

'These pieces reflect a personal interest in a particular place'

Vicki Ambery-Smith, *Untitled*. Silver, red gold, yellow gold, approx. 10 × 15 × 4mm

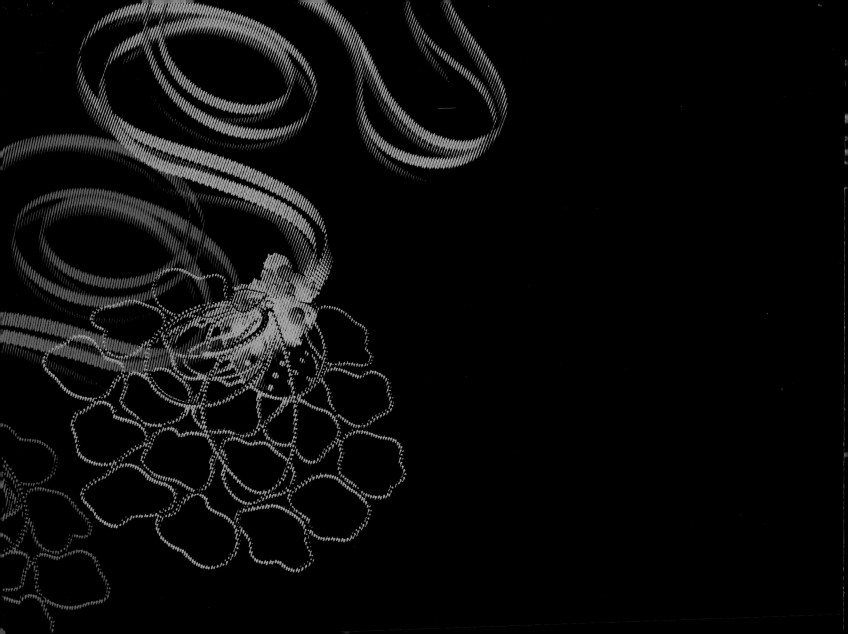

2

Necklaces

A NECKLACE CAN BE
SO MUCH MORE THAN
THE TRADITIONAL
METAL CHAIN WITH
ATTACHED PENDANT.
VARIOUS STYLES OF
NECK JEWELLERY,
FROM CHOKERS, DOG
COLLARS, NECK RINGS,
NECKLETS AND
LOCKETS, HAVE FOR
MANY YEARS BEEN
FORMED FROM A
VARIETY OF MATERIALS.

Necklaces are commonly worn to enhance and accentuate the long, sensual female neck. The giraffe-necked women of tribal villages in Thailand exaggerate this feature by wearing spiral brass rings around the neck in order to elongate it dramatically. As well as displaying beauty and status, in some cultures necklaces are also believed to hold amuletic powers to ward off evil.

In 2006, two marine shells in the collection of the Natural History Museum, London, were identified as beads, artificially pierced for use as pendants or in necklaces. Dated at 100,000 years old, they are the world's oldest known items of jewellery. Primitive necklace construction using materials such as shells, bones, stones, animal teeth and claws strung on thread or leather has been built upon throughout history. Thousands of years

on, contemporary jewellers are still incorporating basic construction methods in their designs. *Brushstrokes* by Hayley Mardon and *Time Line* by Ashley Heminway depict how the marrying of non-precious materials with simple construction techniques can create a stunning piece of jewellery with an understated beauty. Antje Illner simply suspends her glass pendant on a string, thereby exploiting the mesmerizing qualities of a simple glass form.

The earliest necklace made from precious materials is believed to date back to about 3000 BC, and since then jewellery made with precious materials has been widely associated with wealth and status. Ancient Egyptian neck jewellery evolved from simple, strung beads of amuletic and symbolic nature, to spectacular gold collars and pectoral pieces set with gems.

They were worn by both sexes, although mostly only by royals and wealthy citizens, and were often buried with the owners when they died.

The early Romans also buried jewellery with their dead, although at this time the wearing of jewellery was frowned upon and the amount of gold that could be worn or buried was legally restricted. However, this was later relaxed and jewellery was extravagantly worn. As a result, a distinct and recognizable Roman style developed, consisting of substantial coloured gemstones and glass shapes suspended around the neck. Adrean Bloomard, Jacqueline Ryan, Salima Thakker and Andrew Lamb demonstrate how skill and tradition can be utilized to create some dynamic and beautifully executed contemporary responses.

ABOVE: Adrean Bloomard, *Oplontis 6001*.
Oxidized silver, 60 × 25 × 15mm

LEFT: Evert Nijland, *Boccioli di vetro*.
Silver, glass, flock, electric wire, length
450mm

ABOVE: Antje Illner, *2 Pyramids*.
Optical glass, linen, 55 × 35 × 25mm

ABOVE RIGHT: Beppe Kessler, *Turning Point*. Balsawood, gold leaf, glass, cotton, diameter 250mm

LEFT: Angie Boothroyd, *Palm*. 18ct green gold, 22ct yellow gold, 22ct red gold, 18ct yellow fittings, 420 × 5 × 10mm

ABOVE: Barbara Stutman, *Empty Bezel Neckpiece #3*. Coloured copper wire, magnets, 280 × 295 × 16mm

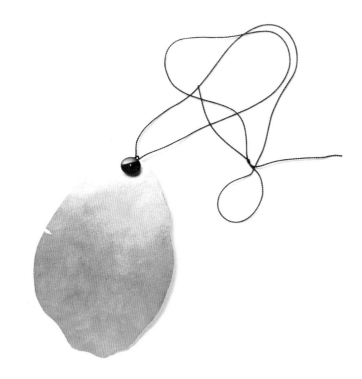

ABOVE: Alison Macleod, *Meminisse*.
Sterling silver, smoky quartz, amazonite,
cherry quartz, ribbon, bra bits, found
objects, approx. 50 × 50 × 35mm

RIGHT: Castello Hansen, *Untitled*.
Fine gold, synthetic ruby, pearl silk,
80 × 120 × 1mm

'Saito's jewellery reflects what she sees in nature'

LEFT: Kayo Saito, *Layer*. Polyester fibre, white metal, magnets, 230 × 100 × 230mm

ABOVE: Alison Macleod, *Victoriana pendant with curiosity*. Sterling silver, amazonite, aventurine, iolite, labradorite, ribbon, diameter approx. 80mm

44

ABOVE: Andrew Lamb, 'Changing Colour'
series. Silver and 18ct yellow gold,
diameter 160mm

RIGHT: An Alleweireldt, *Radish*.
Radishes, diameter 200mm

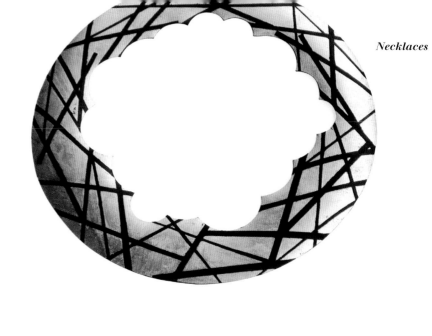

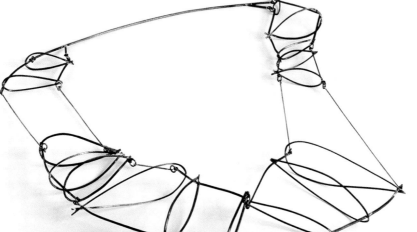

ABOVE LEFT: Carolina Vallejo, *Garden of Eden*. Silver, clay, photos, acrylic, pearl, bone, moonstone, garnet, zircon, gold, bedellium, shoham stone, 330 × 20 × 4mm

ABOVE: Isabelle Metaxa, *Untitled*. Rubber, 24ct gold leaf, diameter 260mm

LEFT: Beate Eismann, *Vockerode I*. German silver, red gold, 290 × 300 × 40mm

ABOVE: Ashley Heminway, *Time Line, Green*. Enamelled copper, sterling silver, leather, 220 × 80 × 5mm

ABOVE RIGHT: Ashley Heminway, *Fragments in Time*. Enamelled copper, sterling silver, 200 × 250 × 10mm

'...echoes of the intense decoration found in Victorian jewellery...'

ABOVE LEFT: Alison Macleod, *Trinkets*. Sterling silver, amazonite, labradorite, garnet, diameter 250mm

ABOVE: David Goodwin, *Flow*. 18ct yellow gold and ruby, 25 × 25 × 15mm

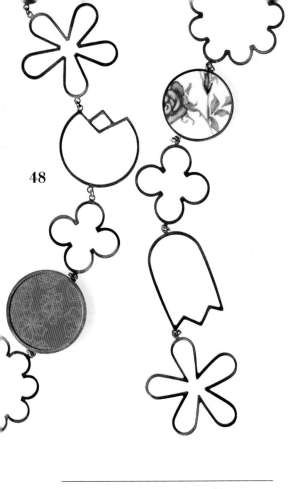

ABOVE: Katy Hackney, *Flower*. Silver,
vintage Formica, 600 × 40 × 3mm

ABOVE RIGHT: Katy Hackney, *Twig*. Silver,
cellulose acetate, Corian, 600 × 40 × 4mm

RIGHT: Katy Hackney, *Nature*. Silver,
cellulose acetate, Corian, 600 × 40 × 4mm

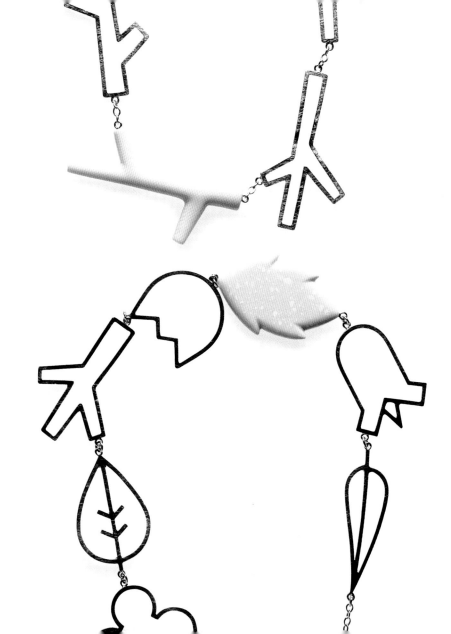

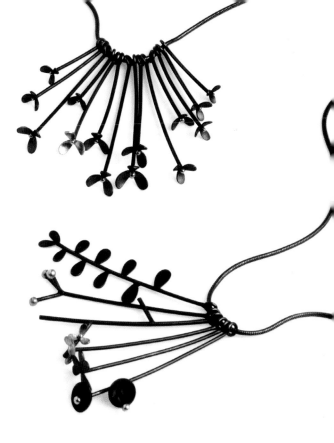

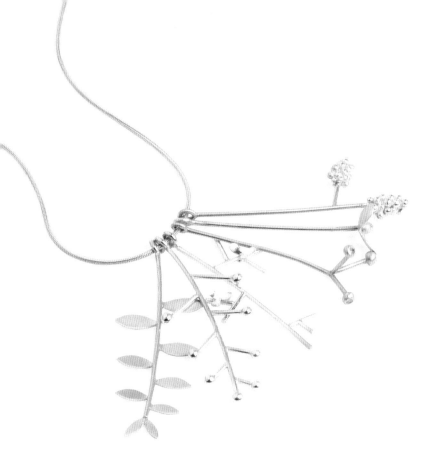

LEFT: Laura Baxter, *Plant Detail*.
18ct yellow gold, approx. 35 × 32 × 6mm

TOP: Laura Baxter, *Flower*.
Oxidized silver and 18ct yellow gold,
approx. 35 × 32 × 6mm

ABOVE: Laura Baxter, *Plant Detail*.
Oxidized silver and 18ct yellow gold,
approx. 35 × 32 × 6mm

50

ABOVE: Hwa-Jin Kim, *Kinder Surprise*.
Silver, aluminium foil, diameter
200mm × 30mm

RIGHT: Kepa Karmona, *Size*. Clothing size
markers, rubber, silver, length 850mm

FAR LEFT: Karin Seufert, *Untitled*.
Plastic, silver, glass, thread, colorit,
PVC, coral, photo, enamel, polyurethane,
diameter 220mm

LEFT: Loukia Helena Richards, *Home*.
Textile, silk thread, cotton threads,
semi-precious stones, coral, button,
embroidered pendant, length 800mm

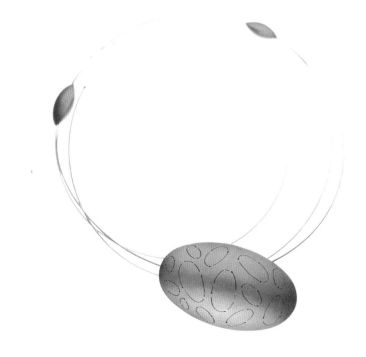

ABOVE: Margareth Sandström, *Concave Blue Oval Rings*. Silver, enamel, length approx. 800mm

ABOVE RIGHT: Margareth Sandström, *Elliptical Bubble*. 18ct gold, approx. 80 × 45 × 20mm

RIGHT: Margareth Sandström, *Boat Cases with Enamel*. Length approx. 800mm

LEFT: Lin Cheung, *Hidden Values*.
9ct gold, 18ct gold, diameter 160mm

ABOVE: Lesley Strickland, *Slot*.
Cellulose acetate and sterling silver,
diameter 170mm

54

ABOVE: Peter de Wit, *Untitled*. Silver, rock crystal, diameter 300mm

ABOVE RIGHT: Daniela Dobesova, interlocking spiral necklace. Silver, 22ct gold, length 630mm

RIGHT: Patricia Madeja, *Cube Chain*. 18ct gold, Tahitian pearls, length 480mm

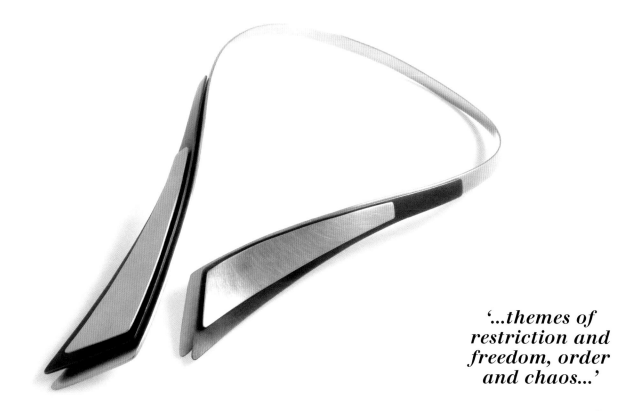

**'...themes of
restriction and
freedom, order
and chaos...'**

Sean O'Connell, *Untitled*.
High carbon stainless steel, mild steel,
$160 \times 190 \times 25$mm

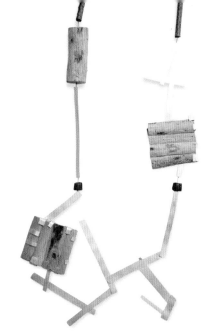

ABOVE: Chus Burés, 'Mae Nam' collection.
18ct white gold, silk thread,
380 × 3 × 40mm

ABOVE RIGHT: Helga Mogensen, *Road-Map
Neckpiece II*. Silver, driftwood, fish skin,
dyed natural material, diameter 915mm

RIGHT: Salima Thakker, 'Modular'
collection. Patinated silver, 18ct yellow
gold, 400 × 50 × 6mm

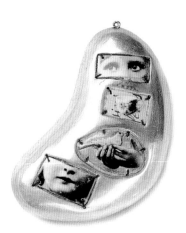

ABOVE LEFT: Carolina Vallejo, 'Esperanza' series. Silver, gold leaf, cotton, photos, acrylic, 70 × 50 × 15mm

LEFT: Carolina Vallejo, 'Esperanza' series. Silver, gold leaf, cotton, photos, acrylic, 70 × 50 × 15mm

ABOVE: Beate Eismann, *Corazón espinado*. Copper, enamel, silver, wood, textile thread, 90 × 68 × 28mm

ABOVE: Rebecca Hannon, *Camino*.
Rubber, 150 × 350 × 0.5mm

RIGHT: Lucy Sarneel, *Ma Blouse Favourite*.
Zinc, textile, rubber, glass beads, gold,
nylon thread, 150 × 350 × 30mm

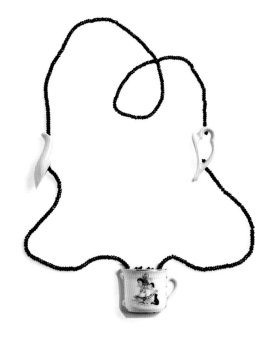

ABOVE LEFT: Mervi Kurvinen, *Benny Hill*.
Silver, plastic, paint, porcelain,
50 × 250 × 30mm

ABOVE: Mette Saabye, *Just Half a Cup*.
Porcelain, lacquer, silver, onyx,
70 × 500 × 25mm

LEFT: Mette Saabye, *The Ideal Couple*.
18ct gold, porcelain, amethyst, chrysopras
beads, 70 × 500 × 30mm

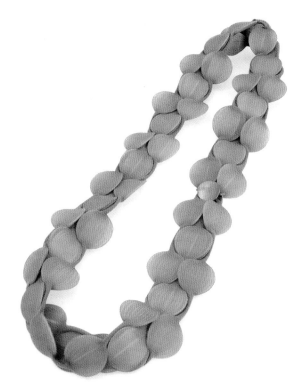

'Ambiguous expression is explored by containing, veiling or wrapping'

ABOVE: Yoko Izawa, *Untitled*. Lycra and nylon yarn, polypropylene, silver, length 600mm

RIGHT: Yoko Izawa, *Untitled*. Lycra and nylon yarn, polypropylene, silver, length 1000mm

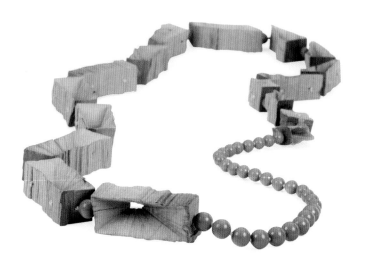

ABOVE LEFT: Stefanie Klemp, 'Erika 05' series. Apple wood, varnish, plastic, length 1090mm

LEFT: Stefanie Klemp, 'Erika 05' series. Apple wood, plastic, thread, length 970mm

ABOVE: Hayley Mardon, *Brushstrokes*. Laminated dyed maple, 22ct gold leaf, blue cord, approx. length 106mm

ABOVE: Lindsey Mann, 'Propeller' series. Printed anodized aluminium, silver, plastics, plastic-coated steel wires, 55 × 45 × 10mm

ABOVE RIGHT: Lindsey Mann, 'Propeller' series. Printed anodized aluminium, silver, plastics, silver cable, 60 × 30 × 10mm

RIGHT: Joanne Haywood, *Torus*. Oxidized silver, textiles, diameter 400mm

LEFT: Tanvi Kant, multicoloured looped rings. Textile, porcelain, length 500mm

ABOVE: Laura Cave, *Advice for Life*. Screen printed and dyed anodized aluminium, 31 × 18 × 1mm

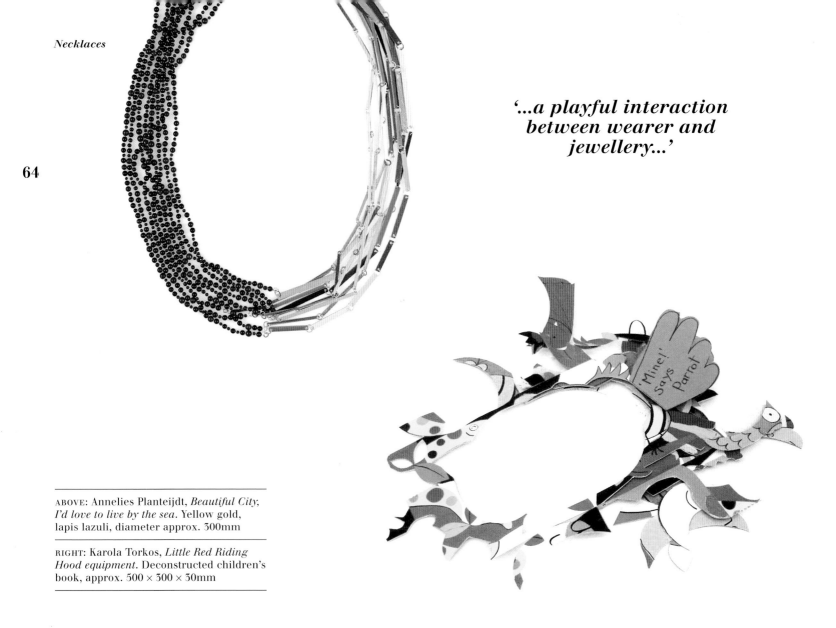

'...*a playful interaction
between wearer and
jewellery...*'

ABOVE: Annelies Planteijdt, *Beautiful City,
I'd love to live by the sea*. Yellow gold,
lapis lazuli, diameter approx. 300mm

RIGHT: Karola Torkos, *Little Red Riding
Hood equipment*. Deconstructed children's
book, approx. 500 × 300 × 30mm

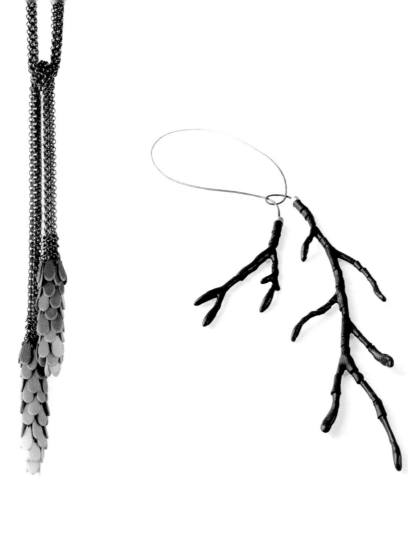

LEFT: Jacomijn van der Donk, *Untitled*.
Silver, old piano key top, length 1000mm

CENTRE: Jacomijn van der Donk, *Untitled*.
Beech twig, epoxy, leather, gold, 1100mm

ABOVE: Jennaca Leigh Davies, *Enamel
Pendant I*. Copper, sterling silver, enamel,
38 × 50 × 38mm

ABOVE: Carla Nuis, *Necklace in C Amorphous*. Charcoal, silk, gold, length 1200mm

ABOVE RIGHT: Gésine Hackenberg, brown Urushi locket. Japanese Urushi lacquer, textile, silver, 18ct gold, 30 × 57 × 18mm

RIGHT: Georgia Wiseman, *Cross*. Onyx, 18ct yellow gold, 440 × 20 × 5mm

LEFT: Pierre Cavalan, *Eternal Flame*.
Mixed media, shell, 95 × 70 × 23mm

ABOVE: Pierre Cavalan, *Heart*.
Enamel, silver, brass, found objects,
120 × 90 × 10mm

ABOVE: Micki Lippe, *Cage Flower*. Sterling silver, 14ct gold, carnelian, garnet, silk thread, approx. 340 × 400 × 40mm

RIGHT: Betty Pepper, *Fairytale*. Textile, silver wire, button, diameter approx. 140mm

LEFT: Bruce Metcalf, *Green*.
Painted maple, holly wood, 23ct gold-
plated brass, diameter 330mm

ABOVE: Bruce Metcalf, *Rhyme and Pun*.
Found objects, iron, 24ct gold-plated
brass, stainless steel, 23ct gold leaf,
305 × 330mm

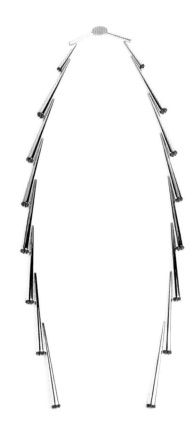

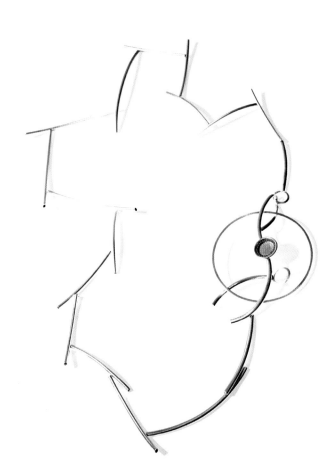

ABOVE: Professor Dorothy Hogg MBE, 'Artery' series. Silver, red felt, length 1500mm

RIGHT: Professor Dorothy Hogg MBE, 'Artery' series. Silver, red beads, length 480mm

ABOVE LEFT: Adrean Bloomard, *Oplontis 4770*. 18ct yellow gold, length 480mm

ABOVE: Elizabeth Galton, *Oriental Sky*. Silver, 240 × 60 × 20mm

LEFT: Elizabeth Galton, *Midas Touch*. 18ct white gold, diamond, 100 × 90 × 20mm

ABOVE: Felicity Peters, *Inspired by the Gherkin*. Silver, rubber earplugs, thread, 60 × 580 × 60mm

ABOVE RIGHT: Hwa-Jin Kim, *Kinder Surprise*. Plastic (Kinder Surprise egg package), 200 × 200 × 30mm

ABOVE LEFT: Stefanie Klemp, 'Erika 04'
series. Apple wood, thread, 6 × 5 × 2.5mm

ABOVE: Mervi Kurvinen, *Steto for Wacko*.
Silver, plastic, satin ribbon, pearl,
140 × 650 × 65mm

ABOVE: Truike Verdegaal, *C'est un oiseau?*
Oui, c'est un oiseau. Gold, silver, amethyst,
length 500mm

RIGHT: Karin Seufert, *Untitled.* PVC, press-
button, onyx, thread, 160 × 300 × 30mm

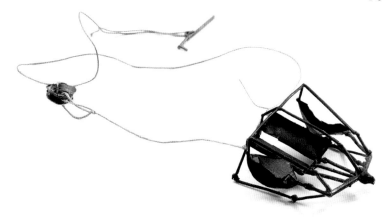

ABOVE LEFT: Inni Pärnänen, *Extraorgans*. Parchment, silk thread, mother-of-pearl, 450 × 75 × 20mm

ABOVE: Andrea Wippermann, *Receiver*. Silver, nylon, approx. 60 × 60 × 50mm

LEFT: Helen Noakes, *Untitled*. Polyester resin, plastic miniature models, silver, 45 × 18 × 18mm

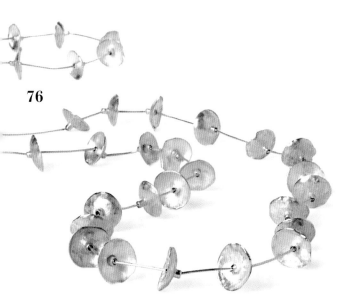

ABOVE: Shimara Carlow, *Articulated Daisy*.
Silver, 18ct yellow gold, length 900mm

RIGHT: Shimara Carlow, silver and paper
dome wrap choker. Silver, silk paper,
diameter 150mm

TOP: Lucy Sarneel, *Mélo-Mélo*. Zinc, textile, rubber, nylon thread, glass beads, paint, wood, 140 × 90 × 35mm

ABOVE: Sonia Morel, *Untitled*. Oxidized silver, length 1400mm

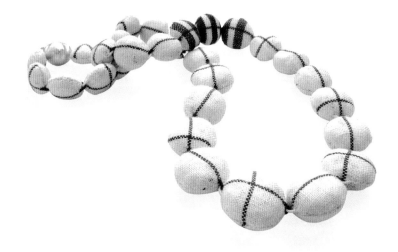

ABOVE: Adrean Bloomard, *Oplontis 3029*.
18ct gold, crushed lapis lazuli, diameter
40mm

ABOVE RIGHT: Gésine Hackenberg, *Kitchen*.
Kitchen towel (linen fabric), silver,
approx. length 650mm

RIGHT: Gésine Hackenberg, *Delft Blue*.
Antique 'Delft Blue' plate (earthenware),
14ct gold, silk thread, approx. diameter
440mm

ABOVE LEFT: Philip Sajet, *Collier Rouge 4*. Gold, waterbuffelhorn, glass, 150 × 200 × 35mm

ABOVE: Terhi Tolvanen, *Birch & Chain*. Smoky quartz, wood, steel, silver, paint, diameter 170mm

LEFT: Terhi Tolvanen, *Swingy*. Hazelnut wood, smoky quartz, silver, diameter 180mm

ABOVE: Tomasz Donocik, *Cossack* scarf.
Silk, gold-plated silver, length 1200mm

TOP RIGHT: Carla Nuis, *Little Potatoes*.
Silver, gold, cotton, length 900mm

RIGHT: Evert Nijland, *Doge*. Glass, linen,
gold, length 700mm

ABOVE LEFT: Loukia Helena Richards, *Cycladic Diamond*. Textile, corals, silk/cotton threads, vintage button, 200 × 300 × 30mm

ABOVE: Ulla and Martin Kaufmann, *Plate*. 18ct yellow gold, 135 × 135 × 0.5mm

LEFT: Ulla and Martin Kaufmann, *Double Circle*. 18ct yellow gold, 145 × 145 × 15mm

ABOVE: Sonia Morel, *Untitled*. Silver, polyester thread, 85 × 90 × 35mm

ABOVE RIGHT: Yeonkyung Kim, *Metal Web*. Fine silver (electroforming), sterling silver, 48 × 62 × 46mm

RIGHT: Hannah Louise Lamb, *Bamboo Wallpaper*. Silver, grasscloth wallpaper, felt, smoky quartz, 60 × 40 × 5mm

'The same elements can be used to explore intrinsically different aspects'

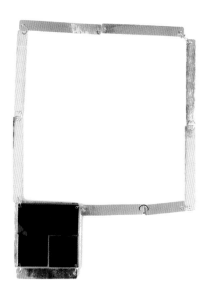

LEFT: Castello Hansen, *Untitled*. Cibatool, 22ct yellow gold, synthetic ruby, diameter 200mm

ABOVE: Annelies Planteijdt, *Beautiful City, view of black*. Yellow gold, titanium, diamond powder, 165 × 120 × 1mm

84

Min-Ji Cho, *Organe* from 'The Gloves'
Dream' series. Rubber gloves,
oxidized silver, freshwater pearls,
200 × 600 × 10mm

'Fresh forms and perceptions of identity'

LEFT: Harriete Estel Berman, *Red Bead Identity Necklace*. Recycled steel containers, Plexiglas, brass, buttons, electrical wire cords, 10ct gold, magnets, approx. diameter 90mm

ABOVE: Dongchun Lee, *Draw*. Iron, 82 × 115 × 2mm

ABOVE: Min-Ji Cho, 'The Gloves' Dream' series. Red (medium) rubber gloves, 18ct gold, shell pearls, 200 × 320 × 20mm

RIGHT: Tina Lilienthal, *Cherry Necklace with Green Gingham.* Polyester resin, silver, ribbon, approx. 40 × 50 × 20mm

'Contemporary notions of value are explored through extremes of precious and non-precious'

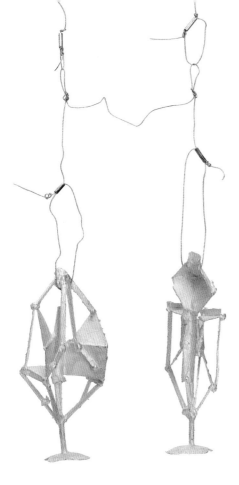

LEFT: Andrea Wippermann, *Das Paar*.
Gold, approx. 30 × 75 × 20mm

ABOVE: Jacqueline Ryan, *Untitled*. 18ct
gold, vitreous enamel, 80 × 42 × 42mm

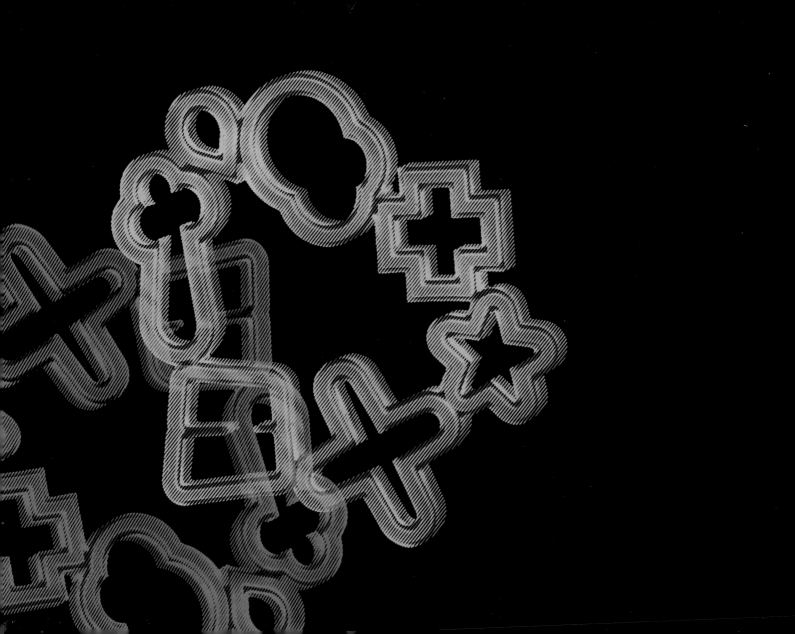

3

Brooches

THE BROOCH IS A
UNIQUE JEWELLERY
TYPE. NOT ONLY CAN
IT SERVE AS A
FUNCTIONAL PIECE,
IT ALSO POSES NO
RESTRICTIONS BY
HAVING TO FIT AROUND
SPECIFIC PARTS OF
THE BODY. ITS ONLY
NECESSITY IS THAT IT
MUST FASTEN TO A
GARMENT, WHICH IN
TURN PROVIDES AN
IDEAL PODIUM ON
WHICH TO DISPLAY IT.

When originally conceived, a brooch's primary function was to fasten clothes. In fact, conventionally, a brooch is still the one jewellery item that retains a function, the mechanics of which have scarcely changed. It wasn't until around the Medieval period that brooches became more decorative and developed into fashion accessories, made with increasingly intricate designs and attention to detail. As with other jewellery, brooches were often symbolic of status. With a pin measure 51.5cm, a tenth-century Penannular thistle brooch found in Cumbria, England, was barely practical as a dress fastener and is likely to have been worn to display wealth.

Brooches were often believed to be amuletic, and were inscribed with words to protect against illness, or with words of religious protection – the name of Jesus was believed to guard against epilepsy. The ring brooch, the most common piece of Medieval jewellery, was quite often given to lovers, inscribed with the giver's intention. A brooch found in Essex, England, amusingly reads 'I am a brooch to guard the breast that no rascal may put his hand thereon'. Today, brooches are still worn to signify allegiances: in recent years they have been adopted by charitable organizations as symbols of support and awareness, the ribbon internationally symbolic of HIV and breast cancer and the red poppy a poignant symbol of war remembrance in the UK.

The practical freedom afforded by the brooch gives creative freedom. Fastened to clothing, the brooch resembles a small canvas on which jewellers can build symbolic references and visually comment on personal observations and cultural concerns. Karin Kato's brooches are symbolic of her childhood while, through the use of synthetic waste and pictures, Kepa Karmona's brooches are representative of political concerns. Terhi Tolvanen's work demonstrates her love of the beauty of nature, while Yeonmi Kang draws inspiration from personal experience to comment on the human condition. Jo Pond's work reflects ambivalent perceptions of beauty, focusing on the vulnerability of imperfection and, in a similar vein, Catherine Truman's pieces consider the perfect and imperfect body. Her work centres on the study of human movement and the history of anatomical representation. Lina Peterson's brooches draw inspiration from their original function, considering the construction of garments and investigating the relationship between jewellery and clothing.

PREVIOUS PAGE: Helga Mogensen, *Golden Chair*. Silver, 18ct yellow gold, driftwood, fish skin, 58 × 50 × 20mm

THIS PAGE: Anna Lewis, *Imprint* pins. Printed suede, silver, vintage buttons, Scrabble tile, 60 × 190 × 20mm

*'Pieces reflecting the
circle of nature bring a
welcome diversion for
city-dwellers'*

LEFT: Deukhee Ka, *Tree Trunk in Autumn*.
Wood, copper, coloured foil,
110 × 105 × 50mm

ABOVE: Alidra Alic Andre de la Porte,
Untitled. Wood and copper,
40 × 60 × 15mm

ABOVE: Adrean Bloomard, *Oplontis 3402*. 18ct gold, sealing wax, 45 × 120 × 15mm

ABOVE RIGHT: Adrean Bloomard, *Oplontis 7009*. Oxidized silver, crushed turquoise, 45 × 110 × 12mm

RIGHT: Francis Willemstijn, *Grief*. Silver, rosewood, 70 × 90 × 60mm

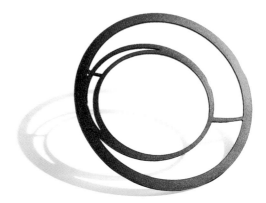

LEFT: Anna Davern, *Large-Breasted Fancy Feather*. Found tea/oil tins, silver, brass, 80 × 150 × 150mm

ABOVE: Rachelle Thiewes, *Mirage*. Steel, kameleon auto paint, 92 × 108 × 7mm

Barbara Paganin, *Fiore di Luce*. Oxidized
silver, gold, brilliants, blown lampworked
green and amber transparent glass,
65 × 100 × 35mm

ABOVE LEFT: Anna Davern, *Milkmaid* (left) and *d'Artagnan* (right). Copper, found biscuit tin, found lolly tin, 35 × 85 × 5mm

ABOVE: Anna Davern, *Beth* (left) and *Pip* (right). Copper, found tea tin, found lolly tin, 45 × 60 × 5mm

LEFT: Jae-Young Kim, *You and Me*. Bamboo, silver, jade, amber, 35 × 100 × 15mm and 70 × 90 × 15mm

*'The choice of material
often reflects cultural
identity'*

98

ABOVE: Kepa Karmona, *Com. Lid*. Cellular
keys, pins, rubber, gasket, cardboard,
optical nuts, silver, steel wire,
75 × 75 × 10mm

RIGHT: Jae-Young Kim, *Early Morning*.
Amber, bamboo, gold, silver, jade,
62 × 52 × 15mm

FAR RIGHT: Jae-Young Kim, *Early Bird*.
Amber, bamboo, gold, silver, coral,
60 × 70 × 15mm

LEFT: Felieke van der Leest, *Jumbo Star Brother*. Plastic, textile, silver, cubic zirconia, 120 × 170 × 70mm

ABOVE: Jo Pond, *So Beautiful*. Vellum, leather, silver, paper, gold, waxed thread, 68 × 150 × 15mm

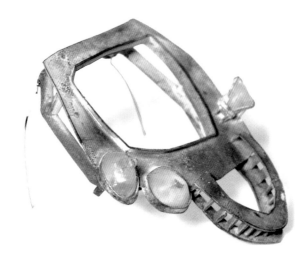

ABOVE: Katy Hackney, *Untitled*. Bamboo, silver, cellulose acetate, formica, wood, steel, 55 × 49 × 25mm

RIGHT: Frederike Schürenkämper, *Untitled*. Silver, synthetic spinell, 70 × 70 × 25mm

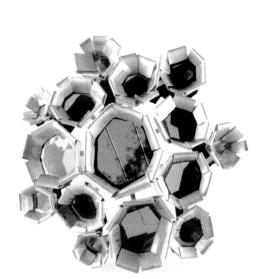

ABOVE: Karin Kato, *It Was Early in the Spring*. Sand, resin, silver, 60 × 110.5 × 40mm

LEFT: Jennifer Howard Kicinski, *15 Heptagons*. Sterling silver, mica, nickel, 63 × 70 × 13mm

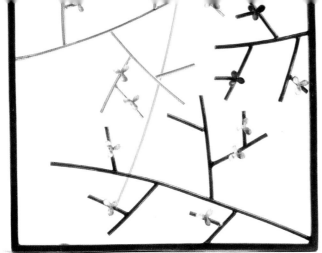

ABOVE: Laura Baxter, *Square Blossom*.
Oxidized silver, 18ct yellow gold,
60 × 60mm

RIGHT: Laura Baxter, *Plant detail*.
Oxidized silver, 18ct yellow gold,
60 × 60 × 5mm

'*Figures and elements
of nature are
abstracted to create
graphic silhouettes*'

ABOVE: Judy McCaig, *Light*. Silver, bronze,
amber, white amber, 54 × 30 × 5mm

RIGHT: Dongchun Lee, *Draw*. Iron,
82 × 92 × 5mm

104

ABOVE: Marianne Anderson, *Pearl Pattern*.
Oxidized silver, freshwater pearls,
diameter 70mm

RIGHT: Sarah Stafford, *Chaos*. 18ct yellow
gold, diameter 50 × 2mm

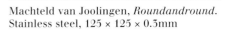

Machteld van Joolingen, *Roundandround*.
Stainless steel, 125 × 125 × 0.3mm

ABOVE: Truike Verdegaal, *Moineau Domestique*. Gold, silver, alpaca, tourmaline, turquoise, lace, wool, 600mm

RIGHT: Truike Verdegaal, *Aigle Imperial*. Gold, silver, alpaca, zirconium, cross stone, lace, wool, 800mm

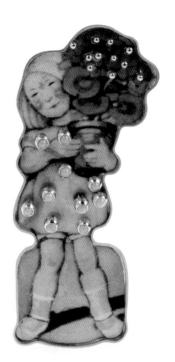

ABOVE LEFT: Terhi Tolvanen, *Aqua Big*. Silver, aquamarine, ceramics, paint, textile, 80 × 10.5 × 110mm

LEFT: Terhi Tolvanen, *Collezione*. Silver, porcelain, agate, labradorite, 110 × 10.5 × 50mm

ABOVE: Mette Saabye, *Cookie Girl*. 18ct gold, scrap and turquoise, 40 × 80 × 10mm

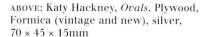

ABOVE: Katy Hackney, *Ovals*. Plywood, Formica (vintage and new), silver, 70 × 45 × 15mm

RIGHT: Katy Hackney, *Untitled*. Plywood, vintage Formica, silver, vitreous enamel, steel, 70 × 30 × 25mm

ABOVE RIGHT: Karin Seufert, *Untitled*. Glass, plastic, rose-quartz, polyurethane, Colorit, silver, steel, 50 × 100 × 15mm

ABOVE LEFT: Jung-gyu Yi, *Lean Against*. Onyx, lapis lazuli, 67 × 56 × 10mm

ABOVE: Jung-gyu Yi, *We Together*. Lapis lazuli, jasper, 925 silver, 72 × 60 × 10mm

LEFT: Jung-gyu Yi, *You and I*. Lapis lazuli, jasper, 925 silver, 60 × 58 × 10mm

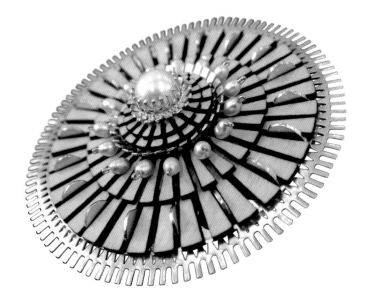

'These pieces explore the relationship between two-dimensional pattern and the three-dimensional object'

ABOVE: Nutre Arayavanish, 'Flourish' series. Plywood, gold-plated silver, freshwater pearls, 550 × 550 × 20mm

RIGHT: Nutre Arayavanish, 'Flourish' series. Plywood, gold-plated silver, freshwater pearls, 400 × 400 × 20mm

ABOVE LEFT: Liz Tyler, *Celebration for the Millennium*. 18ct yellow gold, 0.75ct brilliant-cut solitaire diamond, 2.82cts graduating brilliant-cut diamonds, 50 × 85 × 20mm

ABOVE: Liz Tyler, *Jupiter*. Platinum, 3.15ct marquise tanzanite, 0.20ct trilliant-cut diamond, 80 × 35 × 15mm

LEFT: Marc Monzó, *Big Solitaire*. Silver, zirconia, steel, 65 × 65 × 20mm

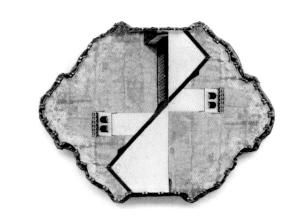

ABOVE: Sebastian Buescher, *Doppelganger*.
Earthenware, silver, wool, goat's tooth,
30 × 90 × 10mm

ABOVE RIGHT: Rebecca Hannon, *Rooftops*.
Photograph, Plexiglas, silver, gold,
40 × 60 × 5mm

RIGHT: Beppe Kessler, *Ups and Downs*.
Balsawood, Swarovski crystals, palladium,
glass, cotton, 35 × 35 × 15mm

ABOVE LEFT: Yeonmi Kang, *Fountain*. Sterling silver, enamel, 24k keumboo/casted, chased, enamelled, fabricated, 40 × 70 × 25mm

ABOVE: Rebecca Hannon, *Neuen Burg*. Silver, Plexiglas, garnet, photo, 70 × 50 × 10mm

LEFT: Rebecca Hannon, *Hirsch*. Silver, Plexiglas, photos, 70 × 50 × 10mm

114

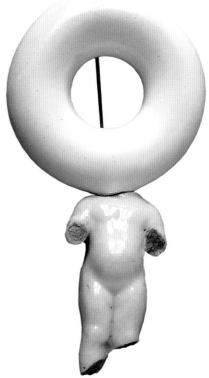

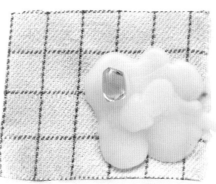

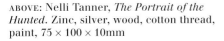

ABOVE: Nelli Tanner, *The Portrait of the Hunted*. Zinc, silver, wood, cotton thread, paint, 75 × 100 × 10mm

ABOVE RIGHT: Karin Seufert, *Untitled*. China, polyurethane, colorit, steel, 38 × 70 × 15mm

RIGHT: Alidra Alic Andre de la Porte, *Untitled*. Cloth, paraffin, lemon quartz, 85 × 70 × 10mm

ABOVE LEFT: Peter de Wit, *Untitled*. Silver, 18ct gold, rock crystal, 80 × 80 × 5mm

ABOVE: Sebastian Buescher, *The Widow Maker*. Earthenware, silver, glass, black widow spider egg cases, cork, poison, approx. 50 × 110 × 50mm

LEFT: Elaine Cox, *Ripple*. Oxidized silver, 18ct gold, haematite, 50 × 42 × 10mm

'*A very specific material takes the foreground*'

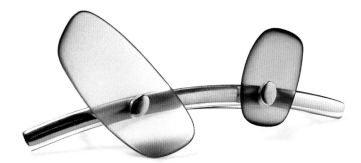

ABOVE: Lesley Strickland, *Jetson*.
Cellulose acetate and sterling silver,
880 × 23 × 5mm

RIGHT: Karin Seufert, *Untitled*.
PVC, thread, artificial leather, silver,
55 × 75 × 20mm

ABOVE LEFT: Lawrence Woodford,
Big Wheel 2. Ebony, 18ct gold, silver,
40 × 40 × 10mm

ABOVE: Daniela Dobesova, *Spiral Arch*.
Silver, 9ct gold pin, 60 × 30 × 20mm

LEFT: Claude Schmitz, *The Falling*. Silver
patina onyx, 85 × 85 × 30mm

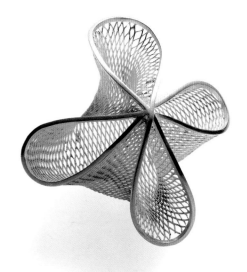

ABOVE: Yeonkyung Kim, 'Metal Web' series. Fine silver (electroforming), sterling silver, 72 × 69 × 45mm

ABOVE RIGHT: Yeonkyung Kim, 'Metal Web' series. Fine silver (electroforming), 18ct gold-plated sterling silver, 50 × 52 × 28mm

ABOVE LEFT: Truike Verdegaal, *Rossignol Philomele*. Gold, silver, laminate, silk, wool, 80 × 210 × 10mm

ABOVE: Professor Dorothy Hogg MBE, 'Artery' series. Oxidized silver, red beads, 100.5 × 100.5 × 10mm

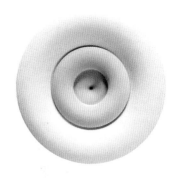

ABOVE: Castello Hansen, *Untitled*.
Cibatool, reconstructed coral, fine silver,
steel pin, diameter 46 × 15mm

RIGHT: Castello Hansen, *Untitled*.
Cibatool, 18ct gold, steel pin, diameter
65 × 15mm

FAR RIGHT: Claude Schmitz, *Nice Place in
Outer Space*. Silver onyx, 65 × 110 × 45mm

ABOVE LEFT: Anna Lewis, *Butterfly* skirt pin. Printed suede, silver, 400 × 500 × 20mm

ABOVE: Carla Nuis, *Potatoes*. Silver, copper, 80 × 50 × 30mm

122

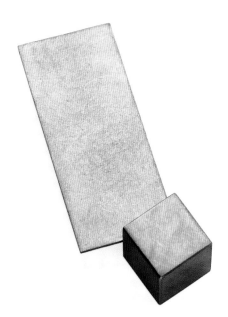

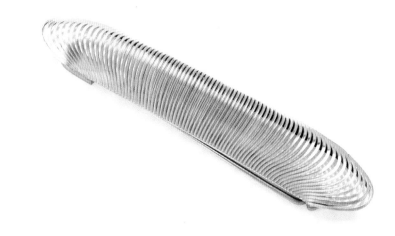

ABOVE: Peter de Wit, *Untitled*. 18ct gold,
20 × 80 × 5mm

ABOVE RIGHT: Andrew Lamb, 'Changing
Colour' series. 18ct white gold,
18ct yellow gold, 57 × 11 × 11mm

RIGHT: Andrew Lamb, *Perspective*.
Oxidized silver, 18ct yellow gold,
35 × 50 × 2mm

ABOVE: Fabrizio Tridenti, *Chs 1*. Oxidized
silver, iron, 100 × 125 × 60mm

RIGHT: Gregor D. G. Anderson,
Composition One. Resin, 70 × 70 × 5mm

ABOVE LEFT: Lina Peterson, *Lesley*.
Plastic dip-coated copper, stainless steel
pin, 70 × 100 × 10mm

ABOVE: Lina Peterson, *Collaged*.
Dip-coated metals and Swarovski crystals,
stainless steel pin, textiles, 80 × 140 × 10mm

LEFT: Lina Peterson, crocheted brooches.
Gold-plated silver and cotton, oxidized
silver and wool, 90 × 80 × 10mm and
60 × 80 × 10mm

126

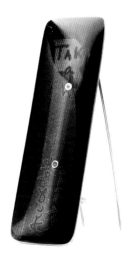

'*Political and social concerns, ideas of exchange and value, expressed through interaction*'

ABOVE: Laura Cave, *Advice for Life – 3 Years On. (What's yer name and where d'you come from?)*. Screen-printed, dyed and anodized aluminium, silver, stainless steel, resin, 60 × 17 × 5mm

RIGHT: Kepa Karmona, *Parada de Emergencia*. Readymade, wooden sticks, cellular keys, silver, steel wire, 70 × 70 × 5mm

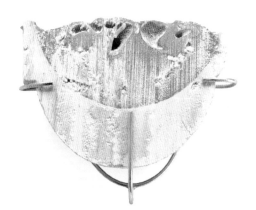

FAR LEFT: Nelli Tanner, *In the Woods II*. Aluminium, elk bone, silver, textile, 45 × 180 × 10mm

LEFT: Zoe Bassi, *Fishing House*. Silver, wood veneer, wood, resin, keum-bu, 78 × 6 × 18mm

ABOVE: Alidra Alic Andre de la Porte, *Untitled*. Silver, plaster, silicone, 48 × 33 × 5mm

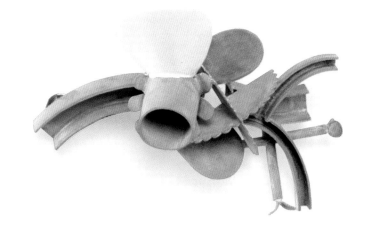

ABOVE: Andrea Wagner, *Satellite City*.
Sterling silver, brass, German silver,
copper, colour-stained unglazed bone
china, polyester granules,
70 × 80 × 30.5mm

RIGHT: Lucy Sarneel, *Pioneer*.
Zinc, paint, silver (pin), 95 × 70 × 40mm

ABOVE LEFT: Andrea Wippermann,
Atico/Pyramide. Gold, 45 × 45 × 10mm

ABOVE: Andrea Wippermann, *Wreck*.
Gold, 60 × 30 × 10mm

LEFT: Daphne Krinos, *Untitled*. Oxidized
silver, diamonds, diameter 72mm

'...jewellery as strange
as it is beautiful...'

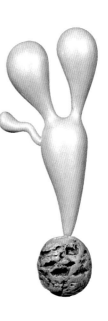

ABOVE: Catherine Truman, *Yellow#1*. Hand-carved English lime wood, painted surface, shu niku ink, 85 × 85 × 35mm

RIGHT: Bruce Metcalf, *Jagrabbit*. Painted maple, 115 × 152 × 10mm

FAR RIGHT: Bruce Metcalf, *Squig*. Painted maple and cork, 45 × 115 × 10mm

ABOVE LEFT: Ramon Puig Cuyàs, *Nocturn* from the 'Walled Garden' series. Silver, wood, plastic, pearl, lapis lazuli, 60 × 60 × 9mm

LEFT: Catherine Truman, *Yellow#3*. Carved English lime wood, painted surface, shu niku ink, 80 × 110 × 40mm

ABOVE: Ramon Puig Cuyàs, from the 'Walled Garden' series. Silver, plastic, wood, onyx, chalcedony, pearl, lapis lazuli, 60 × 60 × 9mm

ABOVE: Jacqueline Ryan, *Untitled*.
18ct gold, approx. 32 × 40 × 10mm

RIGHT: Annamaria Zanella, *Penelope*.
Copper, silver, gold, ebony,
75 × 55 × 13mm

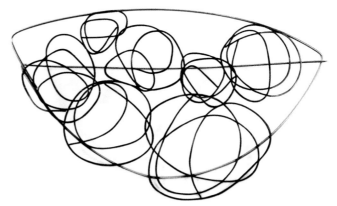

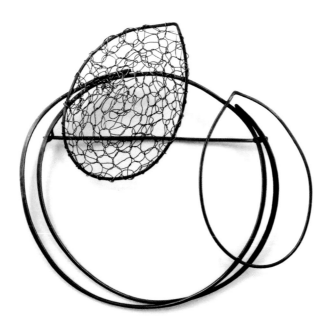

LEFT: Christine Kaltoft, *Chicken Legs*.
Oxidized silver, 70 × 80 × 8mm

ABOVE: Christine Kaltoft, *Coming Out*.
Stainless steel, oxidized silver,
90 × 50 × 8mm

ABOVE: Christine Kaltoft, *Smug Bird*. Walnut, silver, wool, 65 × 68 × 10mm

ABOVE RIGHT: Min-Ji Cho, *Black* from 'The Glove's Dream' series. Rubber gloves, sterling silver, freshwater pearls, 55 × 80 × 10mm

RIGHT: Natalya Pinchuk, 'Growth' series. Wool, copper, enamel, plastic flower parts, rubber grapes, waxed thread, stainless steel, 150 × 120 × 80mm

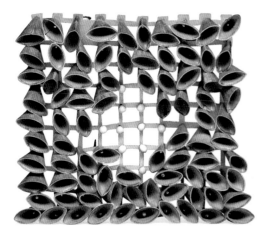

ABOVE LEFT: Min-Ji Cho,
Redrubbercorsage. Rubber gloves,
gold-plated silver, 90 × 90 × 35mm

LEFT: Jacqueline Ryan, *Untitled*. 18ct gold,
vitreous enamel, 60 × 60 × 20mm

ABOVE: Natalya Pinchuk, 'Growth' series.
Wool, copper, enamel, plastic flower
parts, rubber grapes, waxed thread,
stainless steel, 110 × 100 × 50mm

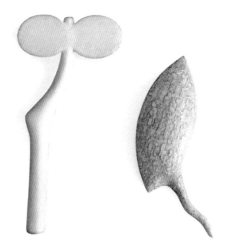

'Experimental materials create intriguing apperances and surface textures'

ABOVE: Hiroki Iwata, *Wish of Leaves & Expression of Plants.* Silver, enamel, gold leaf, 65 × 130 × 15mm and 50 × 110 × 15mm

RIGHT: Andrea Wagner, *House with a White Picket Fence.* Silver, pearls, meerschaum, bone, colour-stained unglazed bone china, 70 × 80 × 40mm

ABOVE LEFT: Castello Hansen, *Untitled.*
22ct gold, acrylic, oxidized silver, steel,
diameter 68mm

LEFT: Lesley Strickland, *Medal.* Cellulose
acetate, sterling silver, 56 × 66 × 8mm

ABOVE: Lucy Sarneel, *Untitled.* Zinc,
antique textile on rubber, wood, silver
(pin), 150 × 110 × 30mm

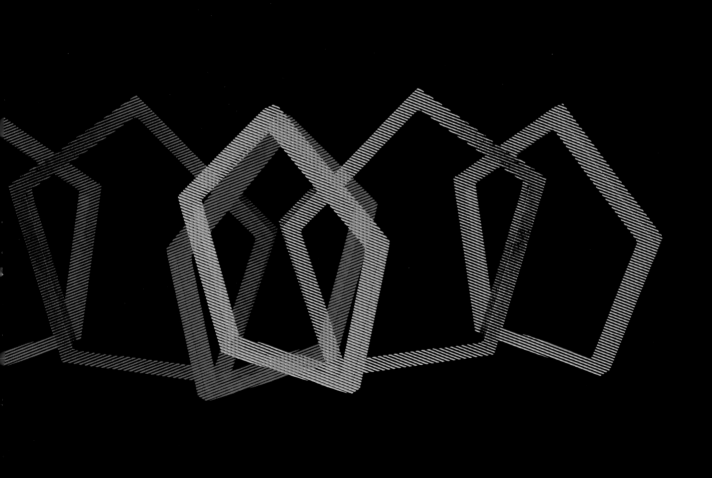

4

Bracelets

AT ITS SIMPLEST, THE BRACELET IS A UNIFYING CIRCULAR FORM WITH NO BEGINNING OR END. WHETHER WORN SINGLY OR IN MULTIPLES, IT PROVIDES THE BASIC STRUCTURE FOR SOME OF THE MOST EXPRESSIVE, SCULPTURAL AND TACTILE PIECES OF JEWELLERY.

Whether a closed circle, hinged with a clasp, a simple string of beads or chain, a charm bracelet, cuff, armlet or bangle, bracelets have adorned the limbs of men and women for centuries. Both wrists of the Venus of Willendorf are decorated with arm rings. Dated at around 25,000 years old, this 11cm-high statuette, discovered in Vienna, is one of the earliest examples of bracelets being worn.

Bracelets are worn not only on the wrist; they can adorn the forearm, upper arm, the ankle and calves. The Ancient Egyptians wore them in multiples – the excavation of Tutankhamun's tomb revealed that the Pharoah was buried wearing thirteen bracelets. The Greeks and Romans also adopted this style, as well wearing bracelets around the upper arm. The term bracelet has its origins in the Latin word *brachium*, meaning 'arm'.

The Ancient Greek adaptation *bracels* referred to the defensive bands of leather, often decorated with gold, silver and gemstones, that Grecian soldiers wore on their forearms. As women began to wear smaller versions, called little *bracels* or *bracel-ets*, the word bracelet was born.

Tying red and white strings around the wrist is a traditional Bulgarian ritual believed to encourage the early arrival of spring. In parts of India the number and style of bangles worn by a woman signifies marital status. Ancient Egyptian bracelets were decorated with motifs or charms to help the gods guide the wearer and their possessions to the appropriate status in the afterlife. In the early twentieth century charms had a dramatic change of purpose when Queen Victoria resurrected the trend for wearing small lockets, glass beads and family crests. From this point

on charms have been worn to symbolize good luck or commemorate significant chapters in an individual's life.

This chapter displays bracelets in a wide range of sizes, from the fine and delicate work of Sonia Morel and Tanvi Kant to much larger pieces, highlighting how contemporary jewellers continue to enjoy the freedom to create on a larger scale. Stephanie Johnson combines delicate textures and natural curves and folds to create bold sculptural pieces. Claude Schmitz creates complex but visually simple structures, while Fabrizio Tridenti builds remarkable pieces inspired by architecture. In Lesley Strickland's work you can see the sculptural influence of artists such as Barbara Hepworth and Constantin Brancusi, and her sensual jewellery forms an essential, tactile relationship with the wearer.

Jo Hayes Ward, *Two-Edge Lace*.
18ct yellow gold, 80 × 80 × 12mm

'...jewellery whose beauty stems from the form itself, rather than relying on decoration or embellishment...'

ABOVE: Daniela Dobesova, *Spiral* bangle with original 'double ball' clasp. Silver patina, diameter 80 × 20mm

RIGHT: Andrew Lamb, 'Changing Colour' series. Silver, 18ct yellow gold, 70 × 90 × 30mm

ABOVE LEFT: Claude Schmitz, *Together 2*.
Silver, diameter approx. 100 × 50 mm

ABOVE: Claude Schmitz, *Ensembles*. Silver
patina, diameter approx. 100 × 50 mm

LEFT: Annamaria Zanella, *Skin*. Silver,
magnet, enamel, lacquer, 75 × 75 × 55mm

ABOVE: David Poston, *Sudan Purée*.
Re-used painted metal from Sudanese
tomato purée tins, wood,
130 × 125 × 55mm

RIGHT: David Poston, *Well, Well, Well*.
Re-used painted metal from black
and golden treacle tins, wood,
155 × 160 × 90mm

ABOVE LEFT: Emiko Oye, *Tansu*.
LEGO®, sterling silver, rubber,
diameter 57.15 × 63.5mm

ABOVE: Harriete Estel Berman, *Tea Column*. Pre-printed steel from recycled containers, plastic, 65 × 105 × 105mm

LEFT: Carole Leonard, *Untitled*. Laminated Perspex, silver, 85 × 85 × 20mm

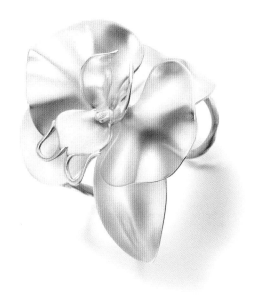

ABOVE: Elizabeth Galton, *Oriental Sky*.
Silver, 70 × 80 × 40mm

RIGHT: Elizabeth Galton, *Titan's Glory*.
Silver, 80 × 60 × 40mm

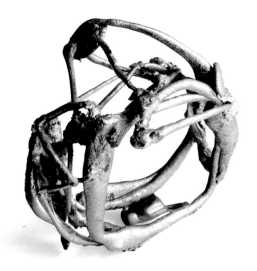

**'...a love of rare
materials, strong
contrasts and extreme
structures...'**

ABOVE LEFT: Fabrizio Tridenti, *Bridge*.
Aluminium, 114 × 85 × 103mm

ABOVE: Francis Willemstijn, *Untitled*.
Bog oak, silver, 180 × 70 × 20mm

148

ABOVE: Joanne Haywood, *Bud Berry*. Oxidized silver, textiles, 10 × 190 × 10mm

ABOVE RIGHT: Barbara Stutman, *Sapphire Duo for a Maharajah*. Vinyl lacing, coloured copper wire, glass seedbeads, 79 × 101 × 70mm

RIGHT: Felieke van der Leest, *Snail-with-Sprouts Train*. Textile, plastic, silver, coral (painted), 225 × 25 × 25mm

Katy Hackney, *Twig & Leaf.*
Cellulose acetate, silver, 180 × 60 × 15mm

'Natural and recycled materials here give organic, sensual vividness and meaningful resonance'

ABOVE: Jacomijn van der Donk, *Untitled*. Silver, goat hair, length 350mm

RIGHT: Fiona Wright, *Evening Standard* bangles. Recycled *Evening Standard* newspaper, diameter 90mm

Harriete Estel Berman, *Antennae/Identity*.
Fossil bronze, black and white UPC,
pre-printed steel from recycled
containers, Plexiglas, brass, polymer
clay, rubber, diameter 180mm

ABOVE AND RIGHT: Marc Monzó, from the
'Hoops' collection. Silver, plastic,
65 × 65 × 7mm

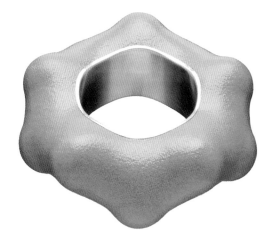

LEFT: Joe Wood, *Lumpy Blue*.
Enamel powder, epoxy resin, silver,
diameter 115 × 50mm

ABOVE: Joe Wood, *Knobby*.
Enamel powder, epoxy resin, silver,
diameter 115 × 50mm

ABOVE: Katja Seitner, *Untitled*. Stainless steel, rose quartz, diameter approx. 70 × 55mm

RIGHT: Katja Seitner, *Untitled*. Stainless steel, smoked quartz, diameter approx. 70 × 55mm

ABOVE RIGHT: Laura Cave, *The Bigger Picture*. Dyed anodized aluminium, rubber, 55 × 55 × 25mm

Patricia Madeja, *Slinky*.
14ct gold, length 190mm

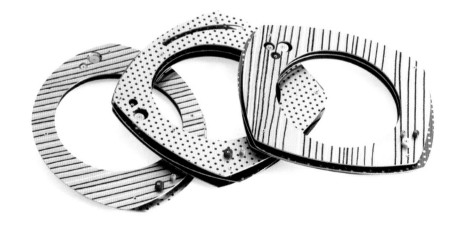

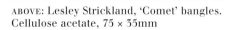

ABOVE: Lesley Strickland, 'Comet' bangles.
Cellulose acetate, 75 × 35mm

RIGHT: Lindsey Mann, *Untitled*.
Printed anodized aluminium, silver ball
bearings, plastics, 100 × 100 × 20mm

Louise Miller, *Bangle and Capsule.*
Acrylic, resin, 150 × 135 × 15mm

Louise Seijen ten Hoorn, *Untitled*.
Silver, diameter 90mm

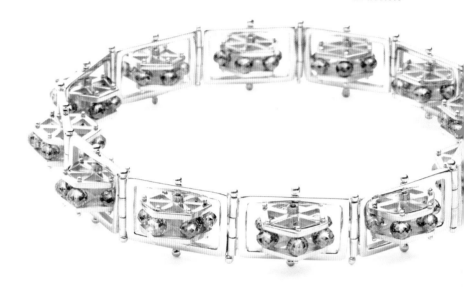

LEFT: Patricia Madeja, *Double Spinning Stone*. 14ct white gold, pink amethyst, length 190mm

ABOVE: Patricia Madeja, *Ferris Wheel*. 18ct gold, champagne faceted diamond beads, length 190mm

ABOVE: Mette T. Jensen, *Untitled*.
Beech and silver, 95 × 95 × 25mm

RIGHT: Mette T. Jensen, *Twin Loops*.
Beech and silver, 100 × 100 × 99mm

TOP LEFT: Rachelle Thiewes, *Mirage*.
Steel paint, diameter 114mm × 42mm

ABOVE: Rachelle Thiewes, *Mirage*.
Steel paint, diameter 114mm × 44mm

LEFT: Rachelle Thiewes, *Mirage*.
Steel paint, diameter 98mm × 54mm

ABOVE: Salima Thakker, from the 'Modular' collection. Patinated silver, 18ct yellow gold, 180 × 60 × 7mm

RIGHT: Salima Thakker, from the 'Grid' collection. Rhodium-plated silver, diameter 630 × 50mm

ABOVE RIGHT: Angie Boothroyd, *Scales*. Suede, 14ct green gold, 18ct green gold, 20ct yellow gold, 22ct yellow gold, 22ct red gold, 9ct yellow gold rivets, 44 × 198 × 5mm

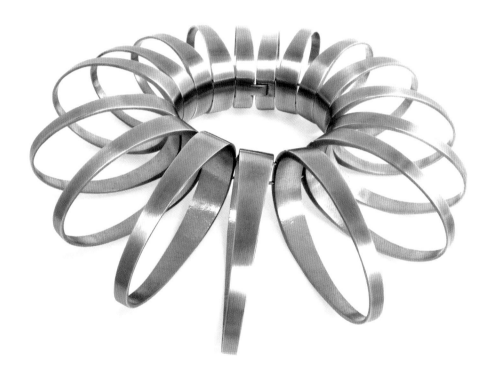

Sean O'Connell, *Untitled*.
Stainless steel, 130 × 180 × 50mm

164

ABOVE: Ornella Iannuzzi, *When Copper is Free from Plastic.* Copper and electric cables, diameter 80mm

RIGHT: Sonia Morel, *Supple and Elastic.* Oxidized silver, 85 × 60 × 85 mm

LEFT: Stephanie Johnson, *Silver Pleat*.
Silver, diameter 68 × 50mm

ABOVE: Gilly Langton, *Loop*.
Silver and red elastic, 100 × 100 × 20mm

166

'The actual making of this work is a core component in its generation, the materials and processes dancing with the ideas and concepts'

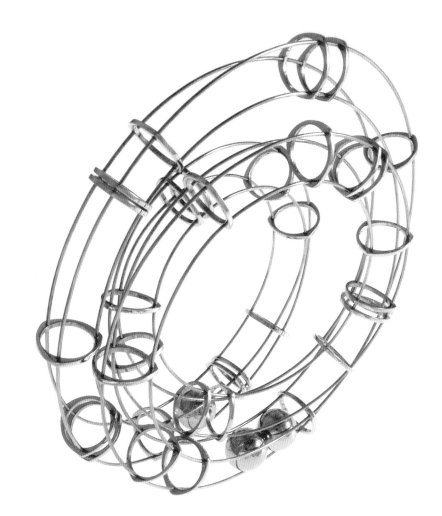

Sean O'Connell, *Winter Crash Tangle*.
Cobalt-chrome alloy, stainless steel,
stainless-steel ball bearings,
160 × 180 × 90mm

ABOVE LEFT AND LEFT: Yoko Izawa, *Untitled*.
Lycra and nylon, polypropylene, silver,
90 × 90 × 30mm

ABOVE: Sonia Morel, *Untitled*.
Silver, steel, 125 × 50 × 125mm

ABOVE: Tamsin Howells, *Multicoloured Wrap Spiral Bangle*. Wallace and Sewell fabric, acrylic, diameter 80 × 60mm

ABOVE RIGHT: Tamsin Howells, *Spotty/Floral Cuff*. Vintage fabric, acrylic, 50 × 100 × 60mm

RIGHT: Tamsin Howells, *Button Cuff*. Fabric, acrylic, 50 × 90 × 50mm

'The simple but
repetitive techniques
used, such as whipping,
binding, knotting and
sewing, transform the
fabrics used'

LEFT: Tanvi Kant, *Multicoloured Flower*.
Textile, porcelain, diameter 100mm

ABOVE: Tanvi Kant, *Multicoloured Ring*.
Textile, porcelain, diameter 100mm

ABOVE: Tomasz Donocik, *Chesterfield Hunters*. Gold-plated silver, leather, sapphires, 70 × 50 × 40mm

RIGHT: Lin Cheung, *Deviated*. Silver, 70 × 80 × 20mm

LEFT: Ulla and Martin Kaufmann,
Mirrored. 18ct yellow gold,
75 × 68 × 35 mm

ABOVE: Ulla and Martin Kaufmann,
Marrit. 18ct yellow gold, 63 × 65 × 60 mm

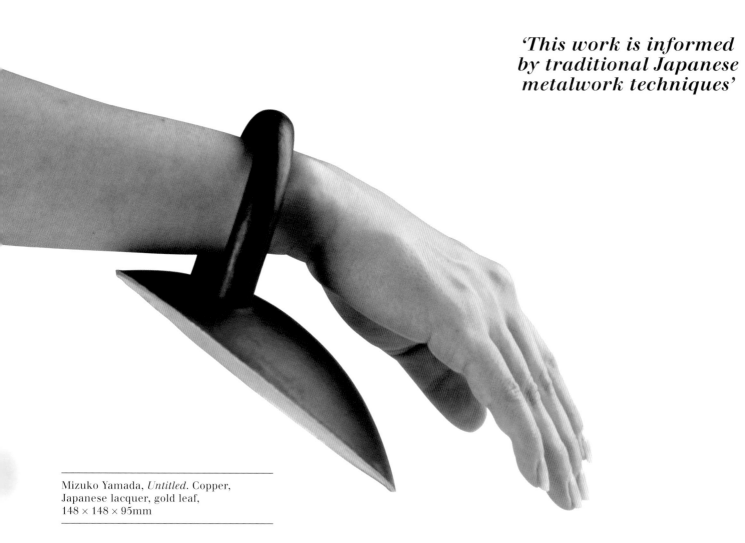

'This work is informed
by traditional Japanese
metalwork techniques'

Mizuko Yamada, *Untitled*. Copper,
Japanese lacquer, gold leaf,
148 × 148 × 95mm

Eun-Joo Noh, *Untitled*.
Copper, wood, paint, 68 × 66 × 110mm

174

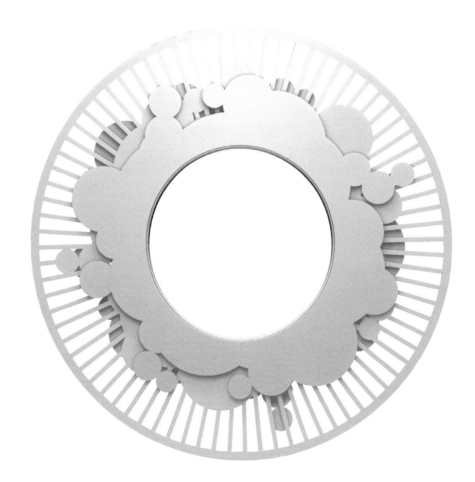

David Watkins, *Cloud Centre.*
Acrylic, diameter 145 × 10mm

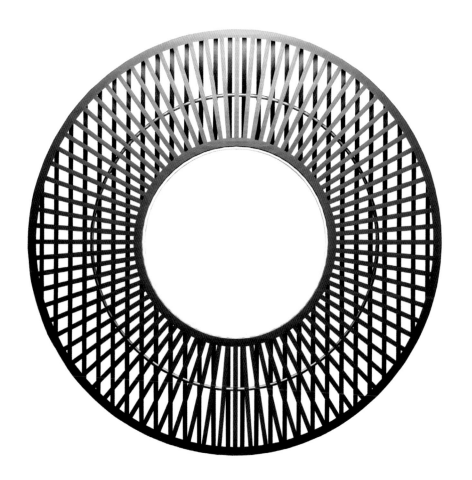

David Watkins, *Suspension.*
Acrylic, gold, diameter 145 × 8 mm

176

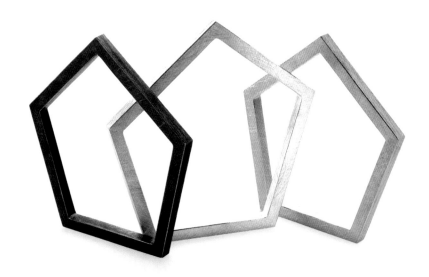

ABOVE: Lawrence Woodford, *Tin Can.*
Silver, 80 × 80 × 30mm

RIGHT: Babette von Dohnanyi, *Vela.*
Silver, oxidized silver, gold-plated silver,
35 × 30 × 7mm

ABOVE: Amanda Mansell, *Untitled*.
Silver, ebony, 300 × 250 × 12mm

LEFT: Amanda Mansell, *Barcode*.
Silver, ebony, acrylic, 350 × 300 × 12mm

5

Rings

THE HANDS AND
FINGERS ARE AN
EXPRESSIVE, FLEXIBLE
AND VERSATILE
COMMUNICATION
TOOL, WITH
THOUSANDS OF
DIFFERENT GESTURES
MADE WORLDWIDE.
IT IS FITTING, THEN,
THAT THE HAND IS
USED TO PRESENT
SOME OF THE MOST
STUNNING AND
DRAMATIC JEWELLERY
PIECES.

The earliest rings are believed to be Egyptian seal rings, used to imprint a wax seal to authenticate documents in lieu of a signature. They are believed to have been worn initially around the neck or arm before they were reduced in size and worn on the fingers. Later, rings were believed to be amuletic, with the power to heal to protect against illnesses. For example, the gem in a Medieval toadstone ring supposedly changed colour if poison was nearby, and rings made of rhinoceros horn were also thought to be an effective guard against poison. Inscriptions and symbols, such as the Shield of David, were also believed to offer protection from injury.

Rings were historically worn on all fingers, including the thumb. Early carvings and portraits, such as *A Young Man at Prayer* (c.1475) by the Flemish artist Hans Memling, show that rings were worn not only past the second joint of the finger as preferred today, but also above it.

In recent times the most common reason for wearing a ring is to mark an engagement, wedding or commitment. This tradition comes from the Romans who gave rings as a pledge of their love. Although the finger on which such rings are worn varies from country to country, the Romans placed the ring on the fourth finger of the left hand, as it was believed the vein from this finger lead straight to the heart – the *vena amoris*.

The rings featured in this chapter are far from traditional, and in the following collection of stunning work you can see how jewellers exploit the hand as a flexible platform from which to display beautiful works of art. They range from delicate to bold and are made for all fingers. In some cases they extend beyond the digit, as with the intricate work of Jieun Park or the curious rings by Hilde De Decker, which encase a growing fruit.

The hand and its jewellery can be viewed from all angles and in various states of movement, an aspect used to dramatic effect in the detailed work of Andrew Lamb. He uses fine lengths of 18ct gold and silver wire, twisted and layered to construct sculptural, three-dimensional jewellery with rippling textures that appear to shift and change in colour with the slightest movement of the hand. The wearer can freely move the ring to experience this effect, engaging fully with the piece.

LEFT: Simone Nolden, *Key-Ring*. Mild steel (part of an iron key), silver, fine gold, star ruby, 24 × 43 × 5mm

ABOVE: Simone Nolden, two 'Nail' rings. Mild steel (iron nails), fine gold, 30 × 30 × 3mm, 23 × 23 × 3mm

*'...capturing the energy
seen in natural forms...'*

ABOVE: Susan May, *Doowop*.
Sterling silver, 38 × 38 × 15mm

RIGHT: Yoko Izawa, *Untitled*.
Lycra and nylon yarn, acrylic, silver, gold,
70 × 70 × 40mm

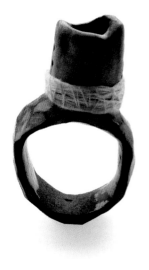

ABOVE LEFT: Andrea Wippermann,
Untitled. Silver, rock crystal,
25 × 45 × 20mm

ABOVE: Sebastian Buescher, *Untitled*.
Earthenware, glaze, thread, approx.
25 × 35 × 10mm

LEFT: Castello Hansen, *Untitled*. 23ct gold,
synthetic ruby, pearl silk, 28 × 8 × 14mm

ABOVE: Monika Brugger, *On the Tip of the Finger*. Thimble, white metal, nickle, silver, 14 × 24 × 14mm

ABOVE RIGHT: Andrew Lamb, from the 'Changing Colour' series. Diamond, silver, 18ct yellow gold, 25 × 25 × 9mm

RIGHT: Carolina Vallejo, *Connection*. Gold, silk thread, 20 × 3 × 300mm

ABOVE LEFT: A-Young Chung, *Tactile II*. 925 silver, iron nail, 45 × 40 × 25mm

LEFT: A-Young Chung, *Tactile I*. 925 silver, steel, 55 × 55 × 25mm

ABOVE: Jieun Park, from the 'Human' series. Copper, 50 × 185 × 50mm

'These pieces are inspired by architectural forms and conceptual art'

ABOVE: Babette von Dohnanyi, *Pentagon*.
925 silver, heat-treated emerald,
35 × 30 × 7mm

RIGHT: Lesley Strickland, *Long Jetson*.
Cellulose acetate and sterling silver,
45 × 32 × 23mm

ABOVE LEFT: Mette Klarskov Larsen, *Last Drop of Blood*. Pre-owned 22ct gold wedding band, human blood, 20 × 23 × 2.5mm

LEFT: Carolina Vallejo, *Happiness*. Silver, glass ruby, 70 × 50 × 50mm

ABOVE: Carolina Vallejo, *Dream*. Gold, glass, cork, lacquer, 120 × 35 × 70mm

ABOVE: Caren Hartley, 'Souvenir' rings.
Silver, vintage postcards, 20 × 20 × 55mm

RIGHT: Caren Hartley, *Picnics*. Silver,
collected receipts, 60 × 55 × 25mm

ABOVE LEFT: Fabrizio Tridenti, *Building*.
Oxidized silver, synthetic enamel,
32 × 48 × 34mm

ABOVE: Sebastian Buescher, *Escape from
Samsara*. Earthenware, plastic, string,
approx. 25 × 40 × 10mm

LEFT: Andrea Wippermann, *Untitled*.
Silver, rock crystal, 35 × 45 × 35mm

ABOVE: Georgia Wiseman, *Captured Tourmaline*. Green baguette tourmaline, 18ct yellow gold, 22 × 32 × 15mm

RIGHT: Claude Schmitz, *Rolling Ring Black*. Silver patina, 35 × 35 × 8mm

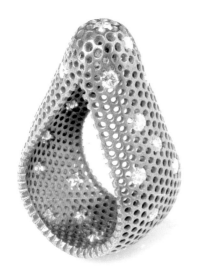

ABOVE LEFT (LEFT): Amanda Mansell, *Untitled*. 18ct white gold, silver, 18ct yellow gold, diamond, diameter approx. 25 × 8mm

ABOVE LEFT (RIGHT): Amanda Mansell, *Untitled*. 18ct white gold, 18ct yellow gold, diamond, sapphire, diameter approx. 23 × 12mm

LEFT: Salima Thakker, from the 'Grid' collection. Rhodium-plated silver, diamonds, 17 × 38 × 15mm

ABOVE: Salima Thakker, from the 'Grid' collection. 18ct yellow gold, emeralds, diopside, 16 × 32 × 15mm

ABOVE: David Goodwin, *Chakra* ring set. 18ct yellow gold, emerald, amethyst, ruby and diamond, 30 × 20 × 30mm

ABOVE RIGHT: David Goodwin, *The 'Ball' Ring*. 18ct yellow gold with diamonds, 35 × 70 × 35mm

RIGHT: David Goodwin, *The Thimble Ring*. 18ct white gold, sapphire and diamonds, 20 × 35 × 20mm

'Repetitious soldering of small units transforms the basic form to dual surfaces with different characteristics'

LEFT: Boosoon Bae, *Untitled*.
Oxidized sterling silver, 30 × 40 × 27mm

ABOVE: Boosoon Bae, *Untitled*. Sterling
silver, oxidized 24ct gold, 30 × 34 × 26mm

'...intricate geometry, executed with perfect accuracy, aided by new technologies...'

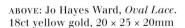

ABOVE: Jo Hayes Ward, *Oval Lace*. 18ct yellow gold, 20 × 25 × 20mm

RIGHT: Chus Bures, 'Living' rings. 24ct gold, 25 × 25 × 3mm

Hannah Havana, *She Loves Me, She Loves Me Not (an engagement ring for the serial fiancée)*. Gilded silver, Swarovski crystal, copper, acetate, 30 × 22 × 25mm

ABOVE: Günter Wermekes, *The One-Carat-Piece*. Stainless steel, 1ct diamond,
23 × 26.5 × 10mm

ABOVE RIGHT: Eun-Joo Noh, *Open the Lid*. gold-plated sterling silver, onyx,
20 × 20 × 33mm

RIGHT: Günter Wermekes, *The Half-Carat-Piece*. Stainless steel, 1ct diamond,
23 × 26.5 × 10mm

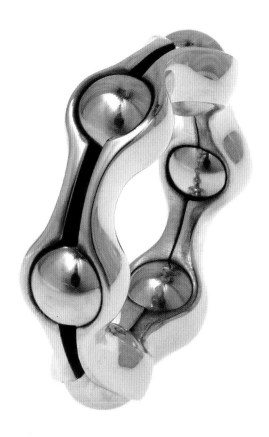

LEFT: Sean O'Connell, *Red Ball*.
375 red gold, stainless steel ball bearings,
28 × 28 × 8mm

ABOVE: Ted Noten, *Design Icon*.
Sterling silver, 19 × 19 × 10mm

ABOVE: Gregor D. G. Anderson, *Turbine*.
Stainless steel, 25 × 20 × 20mm

ABOVE RIGHT: Katja Seitner, *Untitled*.
Stainless steel, quartz, approx.
25 × 25 × 8mm

RIGHT: Jo Hayes Ward, *Tree*.
Silver, 20 × 30 × 35mm

ABOVE LEFT AND LEFT: Sonia Morel,
Substitution. Silver, 25 × 25 × 25mm

ABOVE: Eun-Joo Noh, *Ring*. Sterling silver,
serpentine, 22 × 23 × 26mm

'Geometric forms and architectural structures here express lightness and clarity of thought'

ABOVE: Patricia Madeja, *Tower Ring*.
18ct gold, 3ct cognac colour, raw diamond
octahedron, 7ct diamond baguettes,
cultured Akoya pearl, 33 × 19 × 6mm

RIGHT: Peter de wit, *Untitled*.
18ct gold, 40 × 25 × 10mm

ABOVE LEFT: Peter de Wit, *Untitled*.
18ct gold, 40 × 30 × 10mm

ABOVE: Philip Sajet, *Red House*.
Gold, glass, ivory, ebony, 25 × 25 × 50mm

LEFT: Liaung-Chung Yen, 'Flourishing'
series no. 3. 18ct gold, diamonds, topaz,
22 × 30 × 22mm

ABOVE: Ruth Tomlinson, *Encrustations*.
Silver, found glass, 25 × 20 × 5mm

RIGHT: Ruth Tomlinson, *Encrustations*.
Silver, crystal, porcelain, 35 × 20 × 5mm

ABOVE RIGHT: Kelvin J. Birk, *Round in
Square Ring with Ruby Cluster*. Silver,
rubies, approx. 35 × 30 × 8mm

ABOVE LEFT: Wendy Hacker Moss, *Satori*. Stainless steel mesh, 24ct gold, sterling silver and pearls, 38 × 38 × 25mm

ABOVE: Shimara Carlow, 18ct gold wrap rings. 18ct gold, 25 × 25 × 10mm

LEFT: Shimara Carlow, set of three rings. Sterling silver, oxidized sterling silver, gold, 25 × 25 × 10mm

204

> *'Drawing on the past, found items and historical motifs are given a new personal significance'*

ABOVE: Marianne Anderson, *Rosette*.
Oxidized silver, 18ct gold, 40 × 40 × 5mm

RIGHT: Caren Hartley, *Archive Box*.
Silver, paper, 20 × 20 × 45mm

ABOVE LEFT: Marianne Anderson, garnet rings. Oxidized silver, 18ct gold, oval garnet, 25 × 35 × 7mm

ABOVE: Lawrence Woodford, *Blossom*. Silver, 20 × 30 × 20mm

LEFT: Amanda Mansell, *Untitled*. Silver, 18ct yellow, amber, 25 × 30 × 6mm

206

ABOVE: Margareth Sandström, *Untitled.*
18ct gold, 65 × 30 × 10mm

CENTRE: Margareth Sandström, *Untitled.*
Silver, 150 × 30 × 12mm

RIGHT: Hilde De Decker, *For the Farmer
and the Market Gardener.* Objet trouvé,
tomato, glass container, vinegar,
100 × 150 × 100mm

'...focus on what lies beneath the surface...'

LEFT: BAKS/Kirsten Bak, *Unicated*.
Plane tree, resin, 20 × 20 × 40mm

ABOVE: Hayley Mardon, *Inclusion Rock*.
Dyed sycamore, white metal, enamel,
30 × 45 × 45mm

TOP: Lin Cheung, *Sibling Rivalry*.
Silver, 9ct gold, 20 × 20 × 15mm

ABOVE: Amanda Mansell, *Untitled*.
Platinum, diamond, approx. diameter
20 × 8mm

RIGHT: Amanda Mansell, *Untitled*.
Titanium, fine gold, fine silver, wood
approx. diameter 25 × 6mm

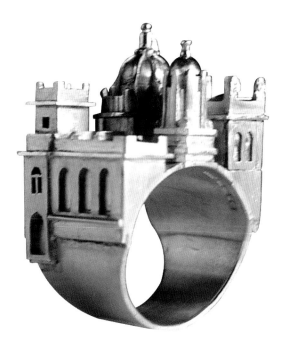

LEFT: Vicki Ambery-Smith, *Oxford*. Silver, red and yellow gold, 25 × 40 × 20mm

ABOVE: Vicki Ambery-Smith, *Tuscan Village*. Silver, red and yellow gold, 75 × 30 × 20mm

210

Mizuko Yamada, *Untitled*.
Silver, blue topaz, 50 × 50 × 30mm

Deukhee Ka, 'Branch' rings. Branch,
copper, colour foil, 925 silver,
110 × 110 × 10mm and 80 × 120 × 10mm

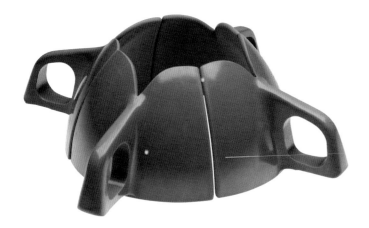

ABOVE: Sarah Kate Burgess, *Set.*
Melamine, 125 × 53 × 125mm

ABOVE RIGHT: Sarah Kate Burgess, *Yellow Spout.* Melamine, 50 × 50 × 64mm

'These pieces suggest that everyday objects are designed as ornaments for the human body'

Lindsey Mann, *Untitled*.
Printed anodized aluminium, silver,
plastics, 23 × 23 × 10mm

ABOVE: Stacey Whale, *Gem of a Seed*.
9ct white gold, 23ct gold balls, sapphire,
22 × 33 × 13.5mm

ABOVE RIGHT: Stacey Whale, *Free Flow*.
9ct white gold, sapphire, fluid,
22 × 33 × 13.5mm

RIGHT: Ulla and Martin Kaufmann,
Architektur. 18ct yellow gold, red
tourmaline, green tourmaline, lemon
citrin, 28 × 25 × 28mm

LEFT: Sarah Keay, gold ring. 9ct gold, monofilament, enamel, 80 × 20 × 10mm

ABOVE: Zoe Bassi, *Buoy*. Silver, gold-plated silver, resin, wood, 70 × 50 × 16mm

*'...small expressions
of art, desire, wit or
sensuality...'*

ABOVE: Ruth Tomlinson, *Encrustations*.
Silver, double pearl, found glass,
porcelain, 60 × 25 × 5mm

RIGHT: Liaung-Chung Yen, *Settled
Situation #1*. 18ct gold, brown diamond,
pearl, 57 × 25 × 45mm

LEFT: Jieun Park, from the 'Human' series. Copper, 120 × 145 × 35mm

ABOVE: Kelvin J. Birk, *Gold Cluster*. 18ct gold, citrine, peridot, tourmaline, approx. 20 × 45 × 10mm

6

Body pieces

THE VERSATILITY
OF CONTEMPORARY
JEWELLERY, IN BOTH
SCALE AND MATERIAL,
ALLOWS ITS ARTISTS
TO MOVE AWAY FROM
CONVENTION AND
DEMONSTRATE SOME
OF THE MOST
PROVOCATIVE AND
DYNAMIC BODY-
RELATED PIECES.

Impressive items of body jewellery have been worn throughout history both for functional purposes and for their powerful symbolic meaning. For example, the Medieval breastplate protected the torso during battle, and a breastplate made from fabric and precious stones was once worn by Jewish high priests. Belts were often elaborately decorated, one example being a Byzantine gold marriage belt embossed with images of Christ blessing the couple. Intricate chatelaines, hung from ladies' belts and designed to hold useful objects, were in high fashion during the eighteenth century, as were highly jewelled shoe buckles. Long Egyptian body chains made of small linked disks were worn diagonally over the body, illustrated by a second-century terra cotta figure from El-Faiyum in Egypt. A similar fashion during the tenth century was a bodice ornament made up of chains decorated with colourful gems, a piece that would have enhanced and covered the entire chest. Elaborately jewelled shoulder clasps from the seventh century were discovered at Sutton Hoo in Suffolk. A vast array of head ornaments and hair decorations have been worn over many centuries and in various cultures, such as the decorated wigs of Egyptian princesses, embellished with a diadem or forehead ornament.

In recent years fashion has provided a stage on which to flaunt contemporary body jewellery. The role of these pieces is not only to accessorize but also to create spectacular show-stopping effects and bold statements. Shaun Leane has produced some sensational catwalk pieces – sculptures built on and around the body – which at times outshine the garments or could even replace them.

Letting the material determine the results, Rowan Mersh uses the body as a blank canvas on which to build sculpturally vibrant pieces, almost disguising the human form beneath. In contrast, Naomi Filmer's work explores and celebrates the body as she focuses on the sensations and relationships between object, material, the body and flesh. Hannah Havana celebrates the body with word play and humour. She adopts everyday objects, transposing their function in witty references to the body, particularly illustrated by *Love Handles* and *Candelabra*.

This is a very brief introduction to a vast area. But this final chapter nonetheless gives a good representation of the overwhelming diversity of contemporary jewellery.

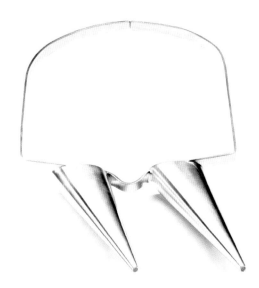

'Humour, wordplay and glamour are used to question the meaning of everyday objects by treating them as precious materials with meticulously crafted finishes'

PREVIOUS PAGE: Hannah Havana, *Candelabra*. Chrome-plated gilding metal, silver, Swarovski crystal, raw silk, found objects, 300 × 300 × 300mm

ABOVE AND OPPOSITE LEFT: Carolina Vallejo, *Envy* (from 'Jewellery for the Sins'). Silver, 200 × 160 × 35mm

RIGHT AND OPPOSITE RIGHT: Carolina Vallejo, *Gluttony* (from 'Jewellery for the Sins'). Gold, silver, porcelain, 80 × 80 × 100mm

OPPOSITE: Ana Claudia Crisan, *Fireveil* (detail, left). Wax and copper wire, 350 × 720 × 300mm

THIS PAGE: Naomi Filmer, *Ice Under-Arm*. Ice, diameter approx. 240mm

Elizabeth Galton, *Orchid Gem*.
Rhodium-plated silver, Swarovski crystal,
180 × 240 × 80mm

Naomi Filmer, *Ice-Upright Hand*.
Ice, diameter approx. 180mm

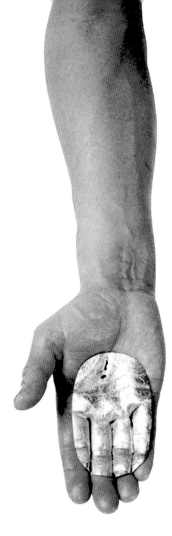

ABOVE: Hannah Havana, *Heels on Wheels*.
Customized rollerskates, stiletto shoes,
glitter, steel, aluminium, rubber,
250 × 110 × 230mm

RIGHT: Carolina Vallejo, *Compassion* (from
'Gesture of the Virtues'). 24ct gold, silver,
70 × 60 × 1.2mm

Emiko Oye, *Cher the Love: Strong Enough Thong*. Recycled Plexiglas, fine and sterling silver, coated copper wire, rubber, 279 × 360 × 30mm

'...jewellery that refers to both folklore and modern iconography...'

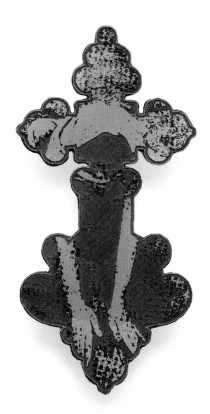

ABOVE: Machteld van Joolingen, *Crying II*.
Stainless steel, elastic, 240 × 120 × 1.8mm

RIGHT: Machteld van Joolingen, *Sisters*.
Stainless steel, silver, 96 × 45 × 1.3mm

Kati Nulpponen, *Fragile*. White clay,
felt; porcelain paint by Tarja Häsä,
80 × 180 × 80mm

OPPOSITE: Rowan Mersh, from the
'External Tumours' series. Knitted
stretch jersey, CDs, 1050 × 550 × 150mm

THIS PAGE: Rowan Mersh, from the
'External Tumours' series. Knitted stretch
jersey, CDs, approx. 650 × 1100 × 150mm

234

Ana Claudia Crisan, *Romance*.
Wax, 790 × 690 × 700mm

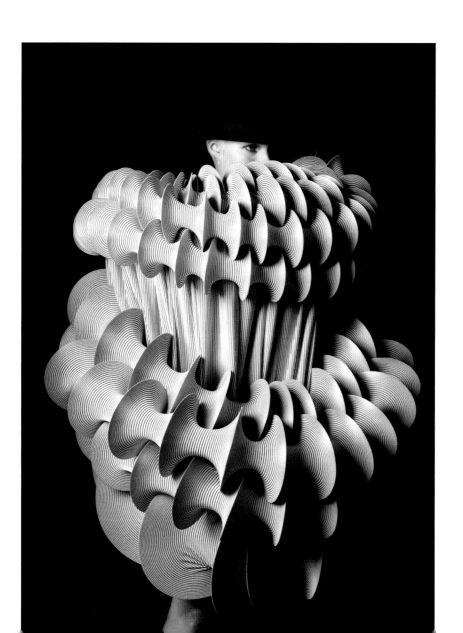

Rowan Mersh, *Vinyl and CD Sculpture Part 3*. Stretch jersey, CDs, vinyls, approx. 1450 × 2300 × 400mm

236

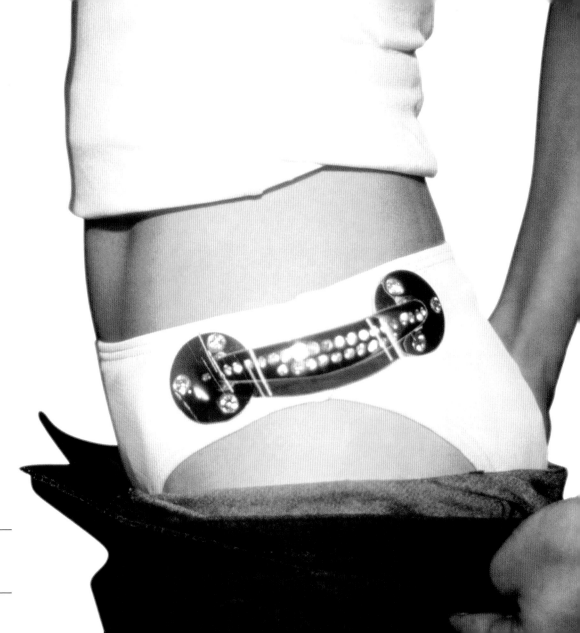

Hannah Havana, *Love Handles*.
Gilded brass handles, Swarovski crystal,
nylon/elastane pants, mixed media,
450 × 190 × 20mm

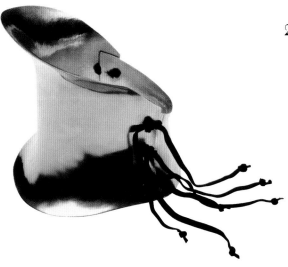

Carolina Vallejo, *Pride* from 'Jewellery for the Sins'. 24ct gold-plated silver, velvet, 130 × 130 × 130mm

OPPOSITE: Shaun Leane, *Silver Body Grid.*
Aluminium, 600 × 300 × 900mm

THIS PAGE: Tine De Ruysser, *Collar.*
Polyester, copper, 400 × 130 × 400mm

Contributors

An Alleweireldt
Belgian
an@oxx.me.uk
www.oxx.me.uk

An Alleweireldt graduated from the Royal College of Art in 2002 and won the Armourers and Brasiers Chambers Award for innovative work. In 2006 she was selected as part of Clerkenwell Green Association's Creative 8 for a solo exhibition in London, which was sponsored by Signity – Swarovski's leading brand on precision-cut genuine gemstones, who supplied her with diamonds – Bellore, Blundells and Sons and Design Flanders. In 2007 she held a follow-up solo exhibition in Belgium.

Alleweireldt's jewellery tells stories beyond appearances, and she likes to combine precious and everyday materials. Her belief is that all objects can live through different lives; it is a matter of how you look at them and what you make of them. Her work is for sale at the Tate Modern, Gill Wing and DualPod, but also through her own website.

Vicki Ambery-Smith
British
vickias@btinternet.com
www.vickiamberysmith.co.uk

Ambery-Smith attended a Foundation course in Oxford in 1973, followed by a three-year jewellery design course at Middlesex Polytechnic. After working as a designer for a manufacturing jeweller, in 1977 she was awarded a grant from the Crafts Council to set up her own workshop. Since then she has exhibited widely and has many pieces in public and private collections, including those at the Victoria and Albert Museum, East Midlands Arts, the Royal Scottish Museum and Houston University, Texas.

Vicki Ambery-Smith has earned an international reputation for her unique style of jewellery based on her interpretations of architecture – ancient and modern – a theme that has developed over 25 years. Some pieces reflect her personal interest in a particular place, while others are based on a building of significance to the client. Her commissions are many and varied, including pieces for the Globe Theatre, Chase Manhattan Bank, Temple Bar, Emily's List Awards and Robinson College, Cambridge.

Gregor D. G. Anderson
British
gregor.anderson@rca.ac.uk

Since graduating from the Royal College of Art in 2005, Gregor Anderson has won runner-up New Designer of the Year and collaborated with leading fashion jeweller Theo Fennell. He has returned to the Royal College of Art, working with the school's digital manufacturing centre, RapidformRCA.

Anderson's jewellery energetically embraces new and challenging technologies and methodologies. He produces innovative and progressive collections in a variety of materials from precious metals to plastics, and for both men and women. His work is the outcome of an investigation into contemporary digital processes and techniques, and his collections explore engineering techniques not commonly found in the jewellery industry, but that complement the work of the studio craftsman.

Marianne Anderson
British
hello@marianneanderson.co.uk
www.marianneanderson.co.uk

Marianne Anderson graduated from The Glasgow School of Art in 2003, and from her studio in Glasgow she exhibits and sells her work internationally. She is interested in how we draw from the past and returns frequently to motifs and patterns of historic and symbolic significance. Her aim is to highlight the importance of ornament in a modern context. Working within a restrained palette of oxidized silver, 18ct gold, red garnets and white pearls, she creates luxurious and wearable collections that skilfully reference the human fascination with adornment.

Alidra Alic Andre de la Porte
Danish
alidra@mail.dk
www.alidraalic.com

After completing her studies in 2006 at the Arti Orafe, Florence, and the Institute of Precious Metals, Copenhagen, Alidra Alic Andre de la Porte has continued to produce jewellery based on freedom of intuition, by playing with materials until they take shape almost by themselves. With a strong emphasis on sensibility, she combines precious metals and stones with textiles, plastic and ceramics.

Nutre Arayavanish
Thai
mail@nutrejeweller.com
www.nutrejeweller.com

Nutre Arayavanish graduated from the Royal College of Art in 2007 and has recently won a number of prestigious awards, including New Designer of the Year 2007 from the Business Design Centre and Jewellery Designer of The Year 2007 (Student Category) from the British Jewellers' Association. She is featured in design magazines such as *Craftsman Magazine*, *craft&design* and *Wallpaper*, and has also participated in a number of exhibitions.

Arayavanish explores the relationship between two-dimensional pattern and three-dimensional object, as well as the relationship between maker, jewellery and wearer, in order to encourage the wearer to engage with more with the jewellery. The pieces are designed to allure and capture the wearer using movement and colour, while exploring the boundaries between jewellery, textiles and sculpture.

Boosoon Bae
Korean
boosoon1@yahoo.co.kr

Boosoon Bae graduated in 2001 from Rhode Island School of Design with an MFA degree with Honours for Jewellery and Lighting Metal, and had her first solo exhibition in 2005.

Her pieces have a tendency not to be flamboyant but always remain quiet and peaceful in experimental ways. She loves to solder, and this allows her to experiment with surfaces and the repetitious soldering of small units. This simple but meaningful process transforms the original form to dual surfaces with different characteristics.

Kirsten Bak
Danish
hello@baks-newjewel.dk
www.baks-newjewel.dk

The 'BAKS UNICATED' collection, designed by the Danish jewellery designer Kirsten Bak, won the Inhorgenta Innovation Prize 2006 and an Award of the Gallery of Art in Legnica, Poland, in 2007. The UNICATED rings have a wooden inner shell and a resin outer shell. Sections of the rings are cut away, encouraging us to focus on what lies beneath the surface and giving birth to uniquely organic yet contemporary shapes.

Bak, who launched her collection in 2006, studied jewellery and industrial design in Germany and Holland, graduating from the Trier Department of Gemstone and Jewellery Design, Germany, in 2005. Her work is a combination of a classic look mixed with an innovative composition of materials and her sculptural collections encourage us to rediscover the shapes and materials that surround us.

Zoe Bassi
British
info@zoebassi.com
www.zoebassi.com

Zoe graduated from Edinburgh College of Art with a First Class Honours degree in Jewellery in 2005. She then went on to complete a postgraduate diploma in 2006.

Her inspiration stems from a childhood growing up near the Scottish coast. Drawings from these areas are translated into jewellery that aims to capture the joy of seaside visits. Colour is an important element in Zoe's jewellery, as well as the different tactile qualities of materials. Since completing her postgraduate course Zoe has moved to Bristol and set up her own studio. Exhibitions include Dazzle, Galerie Marzee and Yorkshire Sculpture Park. She continues to develop her work and undertake commissions.

Laura Baxter
British
enquiries@laurabaxter.co.uk
www.laurabaxter.co.uk

Laura Baxter graduated from Manchester Metropolitan University in 1996. For the past ten years she has built an international reputation for her work through solo and group exhibitions and international trade and retail fairs, including Origin, Chelsea Crafts Fair, Collect at the Victoria and Albert Museum and SOFA in Chicago.

Laura makes precious jewellery inspired by botanical forms. Twigs, buds, blossom and leaf structures are abstracted and magnified at different scales to create graphic silhouettes of nature. The work reflects how plants change and grow throughout the seasons.

Harriete Estel Berman
American
bermaid@harriete-estel-berman.info
www.harriete-estel-berman.info

Harriete Estel Berman uses recycled tin cans to construct artwork ranging from jewellery and tea cups to lawns of tin grass – the latter being conceptual installations, presented as a social commentary on the ultimate consumer icon of American culture. Her work has been shown throughout the United States, and in Europe and Africa and is included in the permanent collections of The Jewish Museum, New York; Jüdisches Museum, Berlin; the Detroit Institute of Art; the Museum of Fine Arts, Boston; the Smithsonian Institution; and the Columbus Museum of Art.

Kelvin J. Birk
German
info@kelvinbirk.com
www.kelvinbirk.com

Kelvin J. Birk lives and works in London and has established an international market for his high quality, innovative, contemporary jewellery, silverware and objects. Birk trained as a jeweller at the Bauhaus-influenced Berufsfachschule for Glass and Jewellery in Germany and at the Sir John Cass Faculty of Art in London.

Over the last few years Kelvin has developed an intriguing collection of work where valuable gemstones are ruthlessly crushed and then reconstructed to create dynamic jewellery and objects. Consciously disregarding what is traditionally considered precious, Kelvin revels in a lack of control, allows chaos to take over and the nature of the precious materials to dictate the final outcome of his pieces.

Adrean Bloomard
Italian
dusiem2@libero.it
www.alternatives.it/GALLERY/E_Bloomard.html

Adrean Bloomard studied metalsmithing at the Art Institute of Rome under Professor Franco Uncini and is co-founder and executive committee member of AGC, the Italian association for contemporary jewellery. His work has been shown in exhibitions and galleries in Italy, England, Austria, Portugal, Japan, Poland, Spain and the United States. He took part in Collect 2007/2008 at the Victoria and Albert Museum and SOFA New York and Chicago 2007.

Bloomard's work is characterized by different textures on the surface of the metal. He is particularly drawn to the warm colour of gold. Oxidized silver and copper are also used in combination with crushed precious stones.

Julie Blyfield
Australian
jblyfield@adam.com.au

Julie Blyfield has her work represented in the major Australian art galleries and in international collections, including the National Gallery of Australia in Canberra; Musée des Arts Décoratifs, Paris; and the Museum of Scotland, Edinburgh. Julie is represented by Galerie Ra, Amsterdam; Galerie Hélène Porée, Paris; and Gallery Funaki, Melbourne.

Blyfield's recent jewellery and vessel work is inspired by collections of botanical specimens. Using mainly pure silver and sterling silver sheet, she creates her jewellery and pieces using the technique of chasing, working the annealed metal sheet with fine steel tools to texture and create surface pattern, taking advantage of the natural distortion occurring during this process.

Apinya Oo Boonprakob
Thai
oopinya@msn.com

Apinya, or Oo, earned a Ph.D. from the Royal College of Art in 1999. Her thesis work, 'Folded Gold Jewellery Collection', won the Nicole Stöber Award from the RCA and the graduate prize from Galerie Marzee in Amsterdam. She is currently a lecturer at Chulalongkorn University in Bangkok, and has continued her research in the area of design and craft knowledge for jewellery.

Oo has set up her own jewellery studio in Bangkok. Her works focus on the perception of the human being in jewellery, the form of her pieces visually unusual for jewellery, but related to the human body when they are worn. Her techniques integrate both traditional and contemporary technologies and reflect the soul of material she selects.

Angie Boothroyd
American
studio@angieboothroyd.com
www.angieboothroyd.com

Angie moved to London from California in 1994 and has been handcrafting her unique style of precious jewellery at her Cockpit Arts studio since graduating from the Royal College of Art in 2001. Angie's work is inspired by a natural sort of geometry, one that allows for natural irregularities, and which truly comes to life when draped on the body. Angie is also something of a modern-day alchemist, painstakingly alloying her golds in the workshop to create a subtle palette of green, yellow and red golds in 18 and 22ct.

Angie has exhibited widely at renowned fairs such as Chelsea Crafts Fair, Origin and Goldsmiths' Fair, and is featured regularly in prestigious galleries such as Electrum and Lesley Craze. March 2008 will see the publication of her first practical book, *Necklaces and Pendants*, published by A&C Black.

Anne Earls Boylan
British
anneearlsboylan@aol.com

Shortly after completing her MA at the Royal College of Art, Anne returned to Northern Ireland to teach jewellery students full-time at the University of Ulster in Belfast. In recent years she has shifted focus back to producing exhibition, commissioned and production work in a range of materials, and now splits her time between teaching and making.

In Anne's work concepts and media are explored in parallel and given form through physical materials. Her influences are social and philosophical, with their origins rooted in a quest to define value. Recent bodies of work have referenced the difficult politics of Northern Ireland, where life has been seen as expendable and identity, based on assumptions, rooted in tribal traditions and symbols.

Monika Brugger
German
monkbrugger@free.fr

Monika Brugger obtained a Masters in Applied Art from the Sorbonne, Paris in 2006 and has since then worked as a jewellery designer and taken workshops and lectures on the subject of modern jewellery.

Monika designs open forms of jewellery that question the human being's place in society and explore the notion of beauty.

Sebastian Buescher
German
seb@sebastianbuescher.com
www.sebastianbuescher.com

Although born in Germany, Buescher spent much of his young life travelling and living in Asia, Malaysia, Japan and Singapore. In 1996 he attended a Foundation Course in Art and Design at the University of Westminster, and graduated from London Metropolitan University in 2003 with a BA in Jewellery. As well as enrolling for the MA in Fine Art in Brighton, Sebastian has also recently exhibited at Collect 2007 and has three solo shows coming up in Amsterdam, Rome and Richmond, USA.

Inspired by ancient, ritualistic jewellery, relics, natural materials and meaning, Buescher's work focuses on the journey and not the goal. The use of ceramic material presents a potential expiration date, meaning that the jewel needs to be worn with awareness, which is a ritual in itself.

Chus Burés
Spanish
chusbures@chusbures.com
www.chusbures.com

In 1984 Chus Burés presented his first jewellery collections to instant acclaim. His work has been exhibited in Tokyo, Paris, London and New York, and his ongoing collection, 'Pieces With Artists', has been exhibited in many contemporary museums and art galleries, including the Venice Biennale in 1990. In 1996 Burés began his long relationship with Thailand, first with a series of workshops to stimulate a new jewellery design consciousness there, followed by various collections based on his experiences in that

country. His collaborations with internationally renowned artists such as Louise Bourgeois, Miquel Barceló, Tobias Rehbergher and Santiago Sierra are expanding rapidly and soon to be exhibited at the Guggenheim Museum, Bilbao, and other museums around the world.

Sarah Kate Burgess
American
contact@adorneveryday.com
www.adorneveryday.com

Sarah graduated from Cranbrook Academy of Art in 2002 and currently teaches at Wayne State University in Detroit, Michigan. Her work has been included in *Metalsmith* magazine and exhibited nationally and internationally.

Sarah makes jewellery that explores contemporary concepts of preciousness, value, authorship and wearability. The 'Cup as Ring' series arose from her assertion that everyday objects – in this case tea cups – are designed as ornaments for the human body. In the 'Do it Yourself-Ring' series Sarah designs rings for anyone to make, highlighting the inherent collaboration between jeweller and wearer.

Shimara Carlow
Irish
shimara@shimara.com
www.shimara.com

Born in a remote coastal area of West Cork, Ireland, in 1979, a childhood fascination for collecting shells, stones, mermaid's purses, feathers and pods found along the seashore has been the inspiration for Shimara's work. She has created a body of work based on pod-like structures using silver, 18ct gold, silk paper and gum nuts.

New jewellery collections include 'Gum Nut', with neckpieces, rings and earrings constructed from both silver and real gum nuts, and 'Honesty', featuring whitened and reticulated silver ovals that resemble honesty leaves, constructed into long articulated neckpieces and bracelets.

Pierre Cavalan
French
piercav@aapt.net.au
www.projectroom.com/pierrecavalan

Pierre graduated from the BJO jewellery school in Paris, and, after travelling the world, settled in Australia in 1981. Before setting up his own studio, Cavalan worked for the Sydney trade jeweller Russell McCullough.

Pierre is interested in jewellery worn by men, especially under pomp and circumstance in the military, religious and royal ranks. His recent body of works, 'We Are More Similar Than We Are Different', is about humanity and humility. Pierre's work is represented by Helen Drutt Gallery in Philadelphia and Gallery RA in Amsterdam.

Laura Cave
British
laura@lauracave.com
www.lauracave.com
www.garudiostudiage.com

Laura Cave has been working with anodized aluminium for over ten years, and has developed highly individual techniques through experiment with print and colour. Graduating from the Royal College of Art in 2002, Laura has worked for Jane Adam at Contemporary Applied Arts and judged awards at the 2007 New Designers and Origin

exhibitions. She has also been working alongside fair-trade jewellery projects in the shantytowns of Lima, Peru.

Laura's work, which has been exhibited internationally, is informed by her interest in working with community groups and exploring ideas of exchange and value. She produces ongoing interactive projects where the audience is involved in the making process and the outcomes go on to form the basis of the next piece. Laura is currently a visiting lecturer at London Metropolitan University and a member of design collective Garudio Studiage.

Lin Cheung
British
www.lincheung.co.uk

Lin Cheung graduated from the Royal College of Art in 1997. The recipient of numerous awards for her jewellery, including The Arts Foundation Award in 2001 and the Deloitte & Touche Award for Excellence in 1997, she is also a respected, published commentator on contemporary jewellery. She exhibits her work both nationally and internationally. Lin has been teaching since 1994, and is currently a visiting lecturer at Middlesex University.

Lin has a profound interest in human nature and is inspired by the social and personal issues that shape our lives; the objects we own, cherish and wear, and our relationships with them.

Min-Ji Cho
Korean
minji@minjicho.com
www.minjicho.com

Min-Ji Cho graduated from the Royal College of Art in 2007 and set up her own studio in London. She has participated in a number of exhibitions, including the International Jewellery Fair in London and Munich.

She has investigated contemporary notions of preciousness by exploring and combining materials that represent the extremes of precious and non-precious. Through using rubber gloves to create adornments she has discovered a new way of looking at found objects in everyday life, interpreting the hidden meaning of real material value as aesthetics of today. In her recent collection, 'The Gloves' Dream' series, she has found boundless potential within the objects and invigorated their use as precious items.

A-Young Chung
Korean
ay7347@hanmail.net
www.myhome.naver.com/chay7347

A-Young Chung graduated as MFA in 2002 from the State University of New York at New Paltz, and studied for a Ph.D. in Metal and Jewellery Design at the Graduate School of Techno Design Kookmin University, Korea. She won the Korea Institute of Design Promotion Prize in the International Jewellery Design Contest. She has participated in a number of exhibitions, including the ENK International Trade Show.

Chung sets a conceptual index on ornaments as tactile objects and likes to use common and cheap materials such as steel nails.

Elaine Cox
British
info@elainecox.co.uk
www.elainecox.co.uk

Elaine Cox graduated from St Martin's School of Art in 1985. Originally trained as an illustrator, her practice is now focused on painting and jewellery. Working primarily in silver and gold, Elaine's work has an organic, sculptural quality, and typically employs richly textured surfaces. She enjoys exploring contrasts: rough with smooth; matt with burnished; light with dark; and precious with non-precious. Her use of unpolished minerals maintains a link with, and celebrates, the materials' origins.

Included on the Crafts Council's list of Selected Makers, in 2007 Elaine was the recipient of an Arts Council England Grants for the Arts Award and a Travel Award from the Association for Contemporary Jewellery. Elaine has exhibited widely throughout the UK and Europe and her work is held in numerous private collections.

Ana Claudia Crisan
Romanian
ana.crisan@alumni.rca.ac.uk
claudia_crisan@hotmail.com
www.claudiacrisan.com

Born in Romania, Claudia came into contact with jewellery during her sophomore year at the University of the Arts in Philadelphia, from where she graduated with a double degree in Metals and Fibers in 2004. This new-found love of material and the interaction between the object and the body sent her to study at the Royal College of Art. Her accomplishments at RCA culminated in winning the 2006 UK Student Jewellery Designer

of the Year. She now owns and runs an Edible Arts gallery/ pastry shop with her husband in Albany, New York.

Her work is ephemeral, soft and feminine, and often includes the use of non-conventional materials such as wax or spun sugar, limiting the length of the piece's life; each piece has a cyclical existence of continuous transformation and movement.

Anna Davern
Australian
annadee@ozemail.com.au
www.annadavern.com.au
www.davernator.blogspot.com

Anna Davern completed her undergraduate degree in Jewellery and Object Design at Sydney College of the Arts, and her postgraduate studies and subsequent Masters degree at the Royal Melbourne Institute of Technology. Anna teaches, writes, curates, blogs and primarily makes jewellery from her studio in Flinders Lane, Melbourne. She exhibits regularly in Australia and overseas, has been the recipient of numerous grants and awards and has participated in residencies in Australia and Europe.

Anna is intrigued by the nature of the relationships that are formed between art objects and a 'viewer'. As a maker of jewellery she is interested in how the process of touching and being touched by art objects enhances these relationships. She is also fascinated by the idea of 'Australian-ness', and plays with cultural stereotypes to investigate notions of national identity.

Jennaca Leigh Davies
American
jennaca_davies@yahoo.com
www.jennaca.com

Jennaca graduated in 2007 from the Rhode Island School of Design with an MFA in Jewellery and Metalsmithing. She also holds two Bachelor degrees from Rensselaer Polytechnic Institute in Architecture and Building Sciences.

Jennaca's inspiration comes from many sources, often based on nature, a unique shape or an architectural detail. She has been exploring new technologies, such as laser cutting and cad cam, while continuing her use of traditional metalsmithing techniques, such as enamelling and fabrication.

Jennaca's work was exhibited at the Talente 2007 exhibition as part of the International Handwerksmesse in Munich. She has received numerous awards, including the Edith and Joseph Alpers Scholarship, the John A. Chironna Memorial Scholarship, and the MJSA Scholarship 2005 and 2006 through the Rhode Island Foundation.

Hilde De Decker
Belgian
hilde@hildededecker.com
www.hildededecker.com

Hilde De Decker studied interior design and jewellery design in Antwerp. Her solo exhibitions consist mainly of jewellery works, but in recent years her monumental compositions have encountered a growing success. These installations give the jewellery pieces an extra dimension as an artistic medium that makes values, techniques and materials secondary.

Since 2000 she has taught at the Gerrit Rietveld Academy, Amsterdam, and gives lectures and workshops at different art schools.

Tine De Ruysser
Belgian
info@tinederuysser.com
www.tinederuysser.com

Tine graduated from the Royal College of Art in 2001. While at the RCA she invented a material that combines the appearance of metal with the flexibility of textile. She is now part of a team funded by the Arts and Humanities Research Council to further develop this material.

Tine won The Armourers and Brasiers Chambers Award for Innovative Work in Metal in 2001, and the Bavarian State Prize in 2004. Articles about her work have appeared in *Hephaistos* magazine, Germany; Kwintessens, Belgium; and kM, the Netherlands.

Nelia de Sousa
Portuguese
info@squarecirclesuk.com
www.squarecirclesuk.com

Nelia de Sousa has been designing and making jewellery for over 11 years, to begin with for an established London-based jewellery design company, and now at Square Circles, the company she established in 2004 with her husband Dyfed Price. Born in Madeira, Portugal, Nelia moved to London when she was 13 years old, and studied at Central Saint Martins College of Art and Design and Brunel University.

Nelia's first collection for Square Circles, 'Doilies', was greatly influenced by her Portuguese heritage, her detailed designs marrying the tradition of embroidery with simple modern aesthetics, resulting in individual, elegant and timeless pieces.

Peter de Wit
Dutch
peter.dewit@telia.com
www.sandstorm-dewit.com

Peter de Wit has moved in the world of geometrical shapes for almost 30 years. His cubes, spheres and cylinders often consist of completely clear or frosted rock-crystal or black onyx and his jewellery expresses lightness and clarity of thought.

Daniela Dobesova
Czech
daniela@danieladobesova.com
www.danieladobesova.com

Daniela trained at The College of Art and Design in her home city of Prague, later continuing her studies in three-dimensional jewellery design at Richmond College of Art in London.

Daniela's designs exploit the properties of shapes and materials to create unique jewellery whose beauty stems from the form itself, rather than relying on decoration or embellishment. The elegant pieces often incorporate innovative clasps and fittings as integral design features. She works in precious metals using self-developed coiling and wire forming techniques, combined with traditional methods.

Daniela's work has won a number of jewellery design awards, and has featured in exhibitions such as Origin, the London Craft Fair at Somerset House, the Royal Academy of Arts, Dazzle and Inhorgenta, Munich.

Tomasz Donocik
Polish
donocik_design@hotmail.com
tomasz.donocik@alumni.rca.ac.uk
www.tomaszdonocik.com

After graduating from the Royal College of Art in 2006, Tomasz worked his first year as a part-time designer for internationally renowned celebrity jeweller Stephen Webster. Tomasz joined together with three other jewellery and silversmith artists and opened Studioeast in London, where he currently operates and designs his jewellery collections. Tomasz has been accredited with several acclaimed awards, including Goldsmiths' Jewellery Designer of the Year 2006.

Tomasz is inspired by literature, architecture and his surroundings. He is interested in new, subtle ways for men to wear jewellery and continuously crosses the boundaries between fashion and jewellery, giving it a new meaning and form.

Beate Eismann
German
jewels@beate-eismann.de
www.beate-eismann.de

Beate graduated from the University of Art and Design Halle, Burg Giebichenstein, Germany, in 1995 and participated in the Mexico Program of the Carl Duisberg Gesellschaft before setting up her own studio in Halle in 1998. She has also worked as an instructor of Basics of Design at the Zeichenakademie Hanau, Germany, and as an art assistant at the jewellery department at Burg Giebichenstein.

As a possible consequence of intensive drawing instruction during her studies, many of Beate's jewellery pieces have a linear nature. Often she produces jewellery that is related to literature, using quotations from novels or songs with the aim of transferring their verbal sensuality into material experiences.

Will Evans
British
Will_evansjewellery@hotmail.com
www.will_evansjewellery@hotmail.com

Will Evans began his jewellery career as an apprentice to a master blacksmith and has since progressed to making highly sophisticated, stylish jewellery. Much of his work has a linear feel to it and his distinctive use of fine gold inlay helps to define, or even defy, the form of the pieces, hence blurring the boundaries between line and three-dimensional form. Will also uses techniques such as folding, forging and soldering precious metals to create striking and unusual shapes.

The majority of Will's work is made to commission and he also produces work for exhibitions such as Goldsmiths' Fair and Dazzle.

Naomi Filmer
British
naomi@naomifilmer.co.uk
www.naomifilmer.co.uk

Naomi Filmer's work explores and celebrates the body, rather than simply decorating it. Her pieces are about the body itself and the physical experience of the wearer.

Naomi holds a Senior Research Fellowship at Central Saint Martins College of Art and Design and has taught in the jewellery and fashion departments of CSM, Royal College of Art, Middlesex University and at the Institute of

European Design, Milan.

Early catwalk collaborations with prolific British fashion designers in the 1990s led to solo and joint exhibitions, notably Be-hind Be-fore Be-yond, Judith Clark Costume Gallery; Jerwood Jewellery, Crafts Council London; Malign Muses/Spectres, Mode Museum, Antwerp and Victoria and Albert Museum; Body Extensions, Musée Bellerive, Zurich; Alchemy: Contemporary Jewellery form Britain, British Council touring the Middle East; and Out Of The Ordinary, V&A. Her work and ideas have appeared in fashion and jewellery publications, including *Fashion at the Edge* by Caroline Evans.

Elizabeth Galton
British
mail@elizabethgalton.com
www.elizabethgalton.com

A graduate of the Royal College of Art, Elizabeth was one of five jewellers nominated for the UK Jewellery Designer of the Year Award in 2006 and 2007. Her collections are sold in prestigious stores in London and throughout Europe, Asia and Russia.

Elizabeth's mission is to bring women around the globe a vision of unique, sophisticated and distinctive jewellery. The myriad forms of her exotic 'Orchids' have become recognizable as her signature motif and her work is synonymous with the finest quality craftsmanship, which embraces the highest standards of creativity and technology. Her jewellery receives coverage in *Vogue, Elle, Tatler* and *Harpers Bazaar*, and celebrity clients include Goldfrappe and Victoria Beckham. High-profile exhibitions include Swarovski's Runway Rocks, New York; Premiere Classe, Paris; and the BFC's London Fashion Week. Corporate

collaborations include work for Mercedes Benz, Cool Diamonds and Swarovski.

Annette Gerritse
Australian

Annette graduated from West Coast College, Carine, Western Australia, in 1998 with a degree in Fine Craft Jewellery.

Working with metals is her passion. To start with a flat sheet and build it into a piece of jewellery, or other object, gives her great pleasure. Her choice of additional materials, be they precious, semi-precious or plain plastic, is based on their ability to serve the creative idea. Some of her pieces might not be primarily wearable, instead they are meant to evoke a smile and exist where jewellery and sculpture cross.

David Goodwin
British
david@david-goodwin.com
www.david-goodwin.com

David graduated from the Royal College of Art in 2004, specializing in the combination of new technologies with traditional jewellery-making practices. David produces work that would arguably otherwise be inconceivable. Inspired by geometry in man-made and natural forms, David's work looks beyond the surface to investigate the underlying structures of objects. Working mainly in 18ct gold, his pieces are studded with diamonds and other precious gems.

David lives and works in London, producing work to commission and for exhibitions such as Goldsmiths' Fair, 100% Proof international touring exhibition and Rising Stars, the 2007 Goldsmiths' Hall summer show.

Gésine Hackenberg
German
mail@gesinehackenberg.com
www.gesinehackenberg.com

Gésine Hackenberg trained as a goldsmith in Germany and studied jewellery design at the Fachhochschule für Gestaltung Pforzheim. She graduated from the Gerrit Rietveld Academy, Amsterdam, in 2001, and has since set up her own studio in the city centre.

She is fascinated by the aspect of personal preciousness that she observes in relation to all kinds of belongings. Her material choices are precious metals, china (shards), textiles and the very tough and resistant Japanese urushi lacquer, materials that catch and preserve a fleeting commonplace culture that surrounds us. Hackenberg's work has appeared in numerous international exhibitions and is included in several museum collections.

Wendy Hacker Moss
American
wendy@wendyhacker.com
www.wendyhacker.com

Wendy earned a BFA in Three-dimensional Media in 1997 and now creates one-of-a-kind and limited-edition jewellery from her studio in Los Angeles, as well as teaching in colleges and universities in the area. Her work has been published in *Metalsmith* magazine and *Lapidary Journal* and books such as *500 Wedding Rings*, published by Lark Books. Her jewellery has featured on television shows and is exhibited in the US and internationally.

Wendy has developed a technique called 'metal origami', in which she folds fine, stainless-steel mesh into tiny flowers, worked and shaped by hand, then securely attaches them to a hand-woven, fabricated, linked or chain-mail base structure. One piece may utilize anywhere from 1 to 3,000 hand-folded flowers, and takes several months to create.

Katy Hackney
British
katyh@mac.com
www.katyhackney.com

Katy Hackney graduated from Edinburgh College of Art in 1989 with a First Class Honours degree, then gained an MA from the Royal College of Art in 1991.

Katy's design decisions and use of alternative materials, such as cellulose acetate, Formica, plywood and enamel paint, are dictated by what she happens upon in thrift stores and reclamation-yard forays. The discovery of an old piece of cellulose acetate or Formica, now no longer produced and therefore extinct, is viewed as others would a costly jewel, squirrelled away until she devises jewellery worthy of it.

Rebecca Hannon
American
rjhjewel@gmail.com
www.rebeccahannon.net

After graduating from Rhode Island School of Design, Rebecca Hannon worked for five years as a goldsmith in New York City, before attending the Akademie der Bildenden Künste in Munich on a Fulbright scholarship. Five years later she returned to the states and currently teaches, lectures and has her own workshop in Ithaca, New York state.

Hannon strives to create evocative objects that double as extremely fine souvenirs. A fleeting memory, a lost bauble or an everyday object can be refashioned to create a small celebratory ornament.

Castello Hansen
Danish
castello.hansen@hotmail.com

Castello graduated from the Royal College of Art 1995 and has since been working full-time with jewellery and related subjects. He has been a senior lecturer in jewellery at Konstfack in Stockholm and a professor at HDK in Gothenburg. He frequently exhibits his work in Europe and around the world.

Caren Hartley
British
caren_hartley@hotmail.co.uk

Since graduating from Surrey Institute of Art and Design in 2006 with a First Class Honours degree in Metalwork and Jewellery, Caren has undertaken a residency at Bishopsland Educational Trust, with whom she took part in exhibitions such as Collect. She is currently pursuing an MA in Goldsmithing, Silversmithing, Metalwork and Jewellery at the Royal College of Art.

Caren is a jeweller whose predominant interest is in objects and what they mean to people. She is excited by items that have been long forgotten about, or seem to have lost their role in life. Recently she has been exploring how these items can be displayed or stored in a way that brings them to the forefront once more and reveals their true personal value.

Hannah Havana
British
hannah@garudiostudiage.com
www.garudiostudiage.com
www.hannahhavana.com

Hannah Havana graduated from the Royal College of Art jewellery department in 2001, and has since been involved in projects spanning all disciplines of art and design.

Initially working for fashion jeweller Scott Wilson, and freelancing as a prop/set maker, Hannah was involved with clients such as Kylie Minogue, Givenchy, MTV and Hugo Boss. This variety of experience is reflected in Hannah's own work, which has been exhibited internationally. She currently works as part of design collective Garudio Studiage, as well as teaching at Central Saint Martins.

The themes that link her work are ideas of humour, wordplay and glamour that question the meaning of everyday objects by treating them as precious materials with meticulously crafted finishes.

Jo Hayes Ward
British
info@johayes.com
www.johayes.com

Constructing jewellery from small, building-block elements, Jo Hayes Ward creates intricate geometric and sculptural pieces with an architectural aesthetic. The complexity of the work and the need for perfect accuracy, particularly with interlocking parts, has led Jo to pursue new technologies. Creating her designs in a virtual environment, Jo employs rapid prototyping technology alongside traditional jewellery techniques. Working with precious and non-precious metals, Jo carefully considers colour and weight in the execution of her jewellery.

Jo, a recent graduate of the Royal College of Art, won the UK's Business Design Centre New Designer of the Year Award in 2006. She is also a recipient of the Crafts Council Development Award. Her work is represented in the Worshipful Company of Goldsmiths' Modern Jewellery Collection and the Alice and Louis Koch Collection.

Joanne Haywood
British
joannehaywood51@hotmail.com
www.joannehaywood.co.uk

Joanne Haywood graduated from Central Saint Martins in 2001, and went on to open her own jewellery studio. Joanne mainly designs and makes jewellery to be exhibited in galleries, but has also worked as a consultant and artist on a variety of commissions in the UK and internationally. As well as being a studio jeweller, Joanne is a lecturer in art and design and has taken part in a wide range of teaching projects and residencies.

Her work draws on the contradiction and conflicts of opposites: skeletal forms and fleshy volumes; natural and unnatural; the absence of colour and the addition of colour; light and shadow; within and beyond control.

Ashley Heminway
British
ajheminway@tiscali.co.uk

Ashley graduated from the University of Brighton with a BA in Contemporary Craft, working with metal, ceramics and glass. Her work has appeared in Jewellery Unlimited, an exhibition and publication collated by the Association for Contemporary Jewellery to reflect the diversity and strength of jewellers working in England. As well as exhibiting collections, she works with individuals to create unique pieces of work based on their experiences and memories.

Ashley's work is predominantly in copper, silver and enamel. Her pieces consist of enamelled imagery with a subtle use of colour and texture. Ashley is the course team leader for the National Diploma in Art and Design at Hastings College, and also works with the craft department teaching metalwork and jewellery to degree level.

Professor Dorothy Hogg, MBE
British
dorothy_hogg@hotmail.com
www.scottish-gallery.co.uk

Dorothy graduated from the Royal College of Art in 1970 and was awarded a Silver Medal for work of special distinction. In 2006 the Royal College granted her an Honorary Fellowship in recognition of her work at Edinburgh College of Art, where she was head of the Department of Jewellery and Silversmithing for 22 years. During that time she curated and organized many exhibitions, both national and international.

Through several decades she has developed new work in jewellery expressing in an abstract way events and changes in her life. The structure and movement of the body with related symbolic thoughts preoccupy her design processes. She works mainly in precious metal and is fascinated by the way forms can be constructed in sheet metal to appear solid when they are in fact hollow.

250

Tamsin Howells
British
jewellery@tamsinhowells.com
www.tamsinhowells.com

After her graduation from Nottingham Trent School of Art with a First Class Honours degree in Decorative Arts, Tamsin continued to design jewellery using plastics and resins. Having explored the properties of trapping handmade embroidered paper in plastic, she went on to combine her love for fashion and textiles by encapsulating various fabrics in the same way, including using damaged vintage fabrics and recycling fabric from men's ties and shirts. Her passion for recycling also led her to use sweet wrappers. These innovative designs won her the British Jewellers' Association Award for Excellence in 2007.

Ornella Iannuzzi
French
ornella.iannuzzi@alumni.rca.ac.uk
www.myspace.com/ornellanaya

After working as a designer for Van Cleef & Arpels in Paris, Ornella Iannuzzi graduated from the Royal College of Art in 2007 with an MA. Whilst at the RCA she developed a unique technique of producing jewellery, by growing her pieces through a process of electroforming. Fascinated by nature and the way things grow, Ornella's interests in science and alchemy – the ancient art of perfecting nature – lead her to experiment with the electroforming process to 'grow' a very tactile range of jewellery. She enjoys experimenting with processes and materials to create unusual pieces.

Antje Illner
German
antje_illner@hotmail.com

Antje graduated from the Royal College of Art in 1994 and is to become a tutor in the jewellery department there. She is also a senior lecturer in applied arts at the University of Hertfordshire.
  Her passion for design is reflected in every area of her professional life and through her research and consultancy, exhibitions, publications and awards. Her recent work as an artist jeweller aims to create a mood of calm sensuality, either visually for the viewer or by touch for the wearer. By holding the smooth, curvilinear shapes the wearer gains a relaxing feeling of refined intimacy.

Hiroki Iwata
Japanese
pongee@jd5.so-net.ne.jp

Hiroki graduated from Tokyo's National University of Fine Arts and Music in 1992 with an MFA in Metal Carving, and has since become an instructor there. She is a member of the Japan Craft Design Association and director of Japan Enamelling Artist Association. She has won a number of prizes in her home country and recent exhibitions include Schmuck, Munich, 2004; 'Collect' at the V&A, 2005, 2006, 2007; and 'Transfiguration: Japanese Art Jewellery Today' at The National Museum of Modern Art, Tokyo, 2007. Public collections include the University Art Museum of the Tokyo National University of Fine Arts and Music; Kyusyu Sangyou University; National Museum of Scotland, Edinburgh; and the Aberdeen Art Gallery, Aberdeen.

Yoko Izawa
Japanese
y_izawa@yahoo.co.uk
www.yokoizawa.com

Yoko graduated from the Royal College of Art in 2003, and has been an artist in residence at the School of Jewellery, University of Central England, since 2004. She has participated in a number of exhibitions, including Collect at the V&A and Origin. In 2007, she was shortlisted for the Jerwood Applied Arts Prize: Jewellery.
Since her MA studies at the RCA, Yoko has been exploring the concept of ambiguous expression by containing, veiling or wrapping. In her objects, elements bound by fine elastic knitting mediate the relationship between the inside and outside of material, and create harmonious forms.

Mette T. Jensen
Danish
me2tejensen@hotmail.com
www.mettetjensen.com

Mette completed her BA (Hons) in Jewellery Design at Central Saint Martins College of Art and Design in 2004, and immediately began work as a self-employed jewellery designer. After two years in London she moved to Denmark, where her jewellery and designs are made in her workshop in Copenhagen, while sold and exhibited internationally.
  When Mette makes jewellery she works with a mixture of precious and non-precious materials; exploring and using the special characteristics each material holds. The inspiration in some cases is the material itself or the way it is normally used, in other cases ideas come from sculptures, architecture and mathematics.

Stephanie Johnson
British
stephaniejohnson6@btinternet.com
www.stephaniejohnsonjewellery.com

Stephanie graduated from Loughborough College of Art and Design in 1980, with a First Class Honours Degree in Silversmithing and Jewellery Design, and began work a year later in a shared workspace, before setting up her own studio in the Lake District in 1986.

A move to Cornwall in 1990 prompted a change in direction with her work, and an award from Arts Council England has enabled her to develop a range of contemporary jewellery that explores the use of pleated and folded silver. Some qualities in her work are a response to patterns and textures observed in nature; others reflect her fascination with contemporary Japanese textiles.

Stephanie's jewellery has been exhibited and sold in galleries and outlets nationwide, and she is a member of the Association for Contemporary Jewellery.

Deukhee Ka
Korean
ibbai1124@hanmail.net

Deukhee Ka graduated from Konkuk University's Graduate School of Crafts with an MA in Metal Crafts and has since worked on various art activities and participated in exhibitions and art fairs at home and abroad.

The main theme of Deukhee's work is the circle of nature, with particular emphasis on the life of trees. She hopes that her jewellery gives city-dwellers a welcome diversion to the hustle and bustle of daily life.

Christine Kaltoft
British
info@christinekaltoft.co.uk
www.christinekaltoft.co.uk

Christine was initially a collector and wearer of contemporary jewellery, while working in a high-powered and challenging job. Deciding to change career, she retrained at the Sir John Cass School of Art, London Metropolitan University. As a maker, Christine found herself using jewellery to capture and reflect less visible aspects of her self and her life.

Christine's current work is based on quick, playful sketches of her pet chickens and also reflects her experiences of rehoming 'spent' chickens for the Battery Hen Welfare Trust. The collection aims to capture a sense of the hens' movement, lightness, volume and essential 'birdiness'. The pieces are made of wood and wire, and employ techniques ranging from crochet to laser welding.

Yeonmi Kang
Korean
ykang3kr@yahoo.com

Born in Seoul, Yeonmi Kang studied at Seoul National University and the University of Illinois at Urbana-Champaign. She has participated in around 60 national and international exhibitions, including two solo shows. Her work has featured in books and magazines, including *Art Jewelry Today* by Dona Z. Meilach, and *500 Brooches*, both published by Lark Books.

The inspiration for her jewellery comes from personal experience, and she explores themes such as dreams and reality, body and spirit, lightness and heaviness of existence and mortality and eternity.

Tanvi Kant
British
info@tanvikant.co.uk
www.tanvikant.co.uk

Since graduating in 2005, Tanvi Kant has exhibited and sold her work in galleries and outlets in the UK and internationally. These include Electrum Gallery, Crafts Council and the Victoria and Albert Museum shop, as well as her solo exhibition – for which she was awarded a travel grant to research materials and techniques in India – and Alchemy, the British Council touring exhibition to the Middle East.

Tanvi creates jewellery using reclaimed textiles and hand-formed pieces of porcelain. The simple but repetitive techniques used – such as whipping, binding, knotting, sewing and constructing units in porcelain – directly influence her work. The process of making develops in response to the materials used. The fabrics are transformed, and in some pieces their original form is visible, allowing the wearer to feel and remember the origins of the work.

Kepa Karmona
Spanish
kepakarmona@gmail.com
www.kepakarmona.tk

Kepa Karmona has a BA from the Universidad Del País Vasco in Bilbao and is a graduate of the Massana School in Barcelona. He currently works as a teacher at the Escuela de Arte y Superior de Diseño in València and organizes workshops on the development of contemporary jewellery for the association Fabrika12, also in València.

Kepa Karmona has shown his works across Europe and the USA. He understands jewellery as

252

a way to share political and conceptual worries, through his pieces made from synthetic waste and used pictures.

Karin Kato
Japanese
karinkato411@hotmail.com

Karin Kato graduated from the Tokyo National University of Fine Arts and Music in 2004 with a degree in Metalsmithing and went on to study at Alchimia, the school of contemporary jewellery in Florence, under Manuel Vilhena and Manfred Bischoff.
  Her work has been featured at the Galerie Marzee, the Netherlands, and at Talente 2007 in Munich. Her jewellery has also been published in *500 Earrings* from Lark Books.

Ulla and Martin Kaufmann
German
ulla-martin-kaufmann@t-online.de
www.ulla-martin-kaufmann.de

Ulla and Martin Kaufmann are fascinated by gold and develop artworks from bands of wrought gold. Their roots are in handcraftsmanship and they have been deeply touched by the artworks of Eduardo Chillida, Richard Serra and Donald Judd, who have devoted themselves to the theme of space. Penetrating this theme and enriching it with the fascination they feel for gold as a material, this couple has articulated their own unique language and simultaneously found their way back to the most essential meaning of the concept of jewellery: to adorn oneself.

Sarah Keay
British
sarahisobelkeay@hotmail.com
www.sarahkeay.com

Since graduating in 2003, Sarah Keay has taken part in numerous international group and solo exhibitions, and gained many commissions, including producing work for Cutting Edge for National Museums Scotland, and a piece of work for HRH The Duchess of Cornwall.
  Sarah's creative practice is heavily influenced by botanical elements, which are recreated and fragmented by units constructed from filament, precious beads, Swarovski crystals and found objects, suspended by enamel. The pieces are designed to allure and capture the wearer using movement and colour, while exploring the boundaries between jewellery, textiles and sculpture.

Sheridan Kennedy
Australian
shri@sheridankennedy.com
www.sheridankennedy.com

Sheridan is a Sydney-based jeweller whose work includes one-off exhibition pieces, retail production, collaborations with fashion designers and design commissions for large-scale public artwork. Her jewellery can be seen in various publications including *Freestyle: New Australian Design for Living*, *21st Century Goddess* and *The Virtual Gallery of Contemporary Jewellery* on CD-ROM. She has exhibited in Australia, China, Japan, the USA and the UK, and her work is in the National Gallery of Australia's permanent collection.

Intrigued by what she calls 'the conspiratorial collusion' between bodies and objects, Sheridan often combines her fascination for kinetic components with her love for the sensual experience of decoration and the pleasures of fashion. Her work explores resemblances between organic and mechanical forms and the seductive interaction between jewellery and wearer.

Janis Kerman
Canadian
jkerman@janiskermandesign.com
www.janiskermandesign.com

Janis Kerman is represented in over 30 galleries around the world and has taught, mentored and delivered presentations on her work both in Canada and the United States.
  In Janis Kerman's studio sketches are meticulously ordered, accompanied by the appropriate stones, and clients visiting the studio for commissions participate in the design process, from inception to finished, wearable jewellery.

Beppe Kessler
Dutch
mail@beppekessler.nl
www.beppekessler.nl

Beppe Kessler graduated from the textile department of the Gerrit Rietveld Academy in 1979. Since then she has worked as a painter and jewellery artist, with many of her pieces featured in museums and private collections.

Jennifer Howard Kicinski
American
jhowardkicinski@yahoo.com
www.jhowardkicinski.net

Jennifer Howard Kicinski earned a BFA in Studio Art at the University of Texas at Austin in 1998 and an MFA in Metalsmithing and Jewellery from the University of Oregon in 2001.

Her work has been featured in national exhibitions and can be seen at Charon Kransen Arts. She is currently president of the Seattle Metals Guild.

Hwa-Jin Kim
Korean
hwajin72@hanmail.net

Hwa-Jin graduated from Kyungsung University with a BFA in Metal Crafts Design and an MFA in Jewellery Design. She moved to Pforzheim in Germany in 1999 where she studied under Wolli Lieglein and Winfried Krüger. Since 2001 she has lectured at Kyungsung University and worked in her own studio, where she likes to combine traditional West African ashanti jewellery techniques and industrial processes.

Jae-Young Kim
Korean
jy723@sookmyung.ac.kr

Jae-Young graduated from Sookmyung Women's University in 1969 and majored in Metal Crafts at Hongik University Graduate School in 1973. She has put on six solo exhibitions in Seoul, New York, Los Angeles and Tokyo, and has been invited to exhibit at more than 50 exhibitions in the USA, the UK, Germany, Japan and Taiwan. She is currently a professor at Sookmyung Women's University as well as a jewellery designer.

Min-Ji Kim
Korean
mjnjek@hanmail.net
www.minjikimstudio.com

Min-Ji graduated from the Royal College of Art in 2006, and while studying undertook a commission for De Beers to make a neckpiece for the Royal Ascot winner's prize. She has also taken part in fashion collaborations for catwalk shows and participated in a number of international exhibitions, including the prestigious Belgian Diamond HRD World Tour Exhibition.

Min-Ji is currently designing her new collection in her studio in Seoul, as well as working on projects for upcoming catwalk shows. Her jewellery combines elements of jeweller's craftsmanship and fashion designer's resources, and gives the wearer the opportunity to experiment with ways of situating it on the body.

Yeonkyung Kim
Korean
studioaura@naver.com

Yeonkyung graduated from the School of Design at Pforzheim University in Germany in 2005. She moved to Seoul in 2005 and set up her own studio, using gemstones to design her unique jewellery. She has participated in a number of exhibitions, including International Jewellery Germany and Korea Competition.

Stefanie Klemp
German
steffiklemp@web.de

Stefanie graduated from the Trier University of Applied Arts in 2004 and went on to work as a self-employed jewellery designer. With her diploma work she won the Graduation Marzee Prize 2004 and the Promotional Prize of the University for Applied Sciences, Trier e.V. She has taken part in several solo, duo and group exhibitions with her collection 'Erika' and the special collection 'BetStefka'.

Stefanie works with the many aspects of the self so that every piece of the 'Erika' collection is part of the whole, like a facet of a person's character. She uses apple wood, which she chops and saws into pieces. The 'BetStefka' collection arises from the interchange of the artistic work of Bety Majerniková and Stefanie Klemp. In exchanging process pieces Bety and Stefanie found a way to express a connection of the two different artistic worlds.

Daphne Krinos
British
daphnekrinos@aol.com
www.daphnekrinos.com

Daphne was born in Greece and came to the UK to study at Middlesex Polytechnic. She established herself as a studio jeweller in the 1980s and has since exhibited her jewellery extensively in several countries. Her work belongs to several public collections and is featured in many books and articles.

She uses metal and translucent stones in her distinctive designs. Her ideas come from looking at buildings, construction and demolition sites, from the stones she usually finds and from the colours of summer in Greece.

Mervi Kurvinen
Finnish
mervi.kurvinen@sci.fi
www.amazinganimal.fi

Mervi is a Finnish artist making contemporary jewellery, jewellery-like objects, installations and video-art. She lives and works in Helsinki and is a member of the jewellery artists' group Amazing Animal.

Mervi's aim is to work conceptually with an open mind, with no need to classify herself into any categories. She gets inspiration from contradictions, such as combining precious with non-precious, and loves kitschy objects that are not useful at all in practice.

Birgit Laken
Dutch
info@birgitlaken.nl
www.birgitlaken.nl

Birgit Laken studied at the Royal College of Art in The Hague and at the Gerrit Rietveld Academy in Amsterdam.

Laken is principally inspired by nature, as illustrated in her 'Mokume Gane', 'Heartwear' and 'Summerland' projects. She gives her jewellery a stilled power by using mainly sober shapes and lines. Laken is currently experimenting with pressing lace into metal to give pieces an aura of nostalgia and a hint of melancholy.

Andrew Lamb
British
lamb_adl@hotmail.com
www.andrewlambjewellery.com

Andrew Lamb graduated from Edinburgh College of Art in 2000. He completed his Masters at the Royal College of Art in 2004 and now exhibits his jewellery worldwide, with work featuring in prestigious public collections in the UK and abroad.

Illusion and the mesmerizing visual effects of Optical Art are significant influences in Andrew's jewellery. By incorporating these principals his aim is to create striking yet delicately shaped pieces that appear to shift and change as the eye moves across them. Andrew also finds inspiration in the linear patterns and structures abundant in nature and woven textiles. With these in mind, he uses a combination of fine lengths of 18ct gold and silver wire to construct sculptural, three-dimensional jewellery. The wire is layered, twisted or overlapped to create pieces with rippling textures and subtle colour changes with just the slightest of movements.

Hannah Louise Lamb
British
hannah@itchyfingers.org
www.itchyfingers.org

Since graduating from Glasgow School of Art in 2000 and The Royal College of Art in 2004, Hannah has worked from a shared studio in Edinburgh.

A sense of beauty and perfection, an eye for detail and a strong sense of place all combine in Lamb's jewellery to create unique, highly desirable and wearable pieces. Decorative motifs

and colours from wall coverings and interior fabrics, pets and simple iconic imagery from around the house inform elements of her designs. Techniques used are intricate hand piercing, surface texturing and traditional jewellery fabrication skills combining silver with materials such as silk, felt and semi-precious stones.

Gilly Langton
British
gillylangton@hotmail.com
www.gillylangton.co.uk

Gilly is a silversmith and jewellery graduate from Loughborough College of Art and Design and has been running her own business for ten years. She has exhibited widely in the UK and abroad including SOFA, Chicago; Object Gallery, Sydney; London Fashion Week; and Chelsea Craft Fairs.

Gilly is a contemporary jewellery designer with an architecturally inspired aesthetic that naturally revels in smooth shape and elegant form. Clean, modernist lines contrast with the fine human craftsmanship and subtle detailing that is intrinsic in all of her designs. She combines silver, enamel and coloured elastic to create her bold pieces.

Mette Klarskov Larsen
Danish
m.klarskov-larsen@alumni.rca.ac.uk
www.metteklarskovlarsen.com

Having recently graduated from the Royal College of Art, Mette creates jewellery that reflects a continuous research into lived experiences, uncovering and discovering new layers of human complexity. Taking her inspiration from real-life stories via interviews and newspaper cuttings, her work challenges the notion of jewellery in contemporary culture. The intellectual engagement between story and piece is fundamental in order for it to become part of a broader social context. The idea behind a piece informs the choice of material, scale and form.

Shaun Leane
British
info@shaunleane.com
www.shaunleane.com

Trained in Hatton Garden, London's jewellery quarter, Shaun Leane is a member of the Institute of Professional Goldsmiths. Awarded UK Jewellery Designer of the Year 2004 and 2005, Shaun Leane is internationally celebrated for pushing the boundaries of jewellery design. In 2005 Shaun released his first full diamond collection in celebration of his twentieth year in the jewellery industry. In 2006 Shaun was granted Freemanship of the City of London for his contribution to the UK jewellery industry.

Alongside his collections and bespoke pieces, Shaun also creates some of the most iconic catwalk pieces seen today. Past catwalk collaborations have included acclaimed projects with Alexander McQueen, Marc Jacobs, Givenchy and artist Sam Taylor Wood.

Dongchun Lee
Korean
jewelee@kookmin.ac.kr

Dongchun Lee received his BFA in 1992 from Kookmin University, Seoul and in 1998 graduated from Fachhochschule Pforzheim. He began his career as a jewellery designer in Germany and is now a professor in the Department of Metalwork and Jewellery at Kookmin University.

Dongchun concentrates on using iron, its inconvenience transforming jewellery into something attractive by embracing time, while the time that it captures may deprive the form. His works show abstract figurations of the human body that search for another form of line and surface in association with the figure. Dongchun believes that modern jewellery requires exchanges of emotional and intellectual thoughts between artists and wearers, thus conversation between the artist, wearer and jewellery is crucial.

Hongsock Lee
Korean
arshong@hotmail.com
www.arshong.com

Hongsock Lee graduated from Rhode Island School of Design in 2003, after which time he worked as a jewellery designer for a company and taught at the school. He has now established his own studio in Pawtucket, Rhode Island, where he designs and makes his unique geometric jewellery and sculpture.
Lee has exhibited widely in the US and received several awards.

Florence Lehmann
French
florence.lehmann@free.fr

Florence Lehmann graduated from the Ecole Supérieure des Arts Décoratifs, Strasbourg in 1987 and has been teaching and designing contemporary jewellery ever since. Her work has been exhibited in galleries and museums throughout Europe and is in the permanent collections of the Musée des Arts Décoratifs in

Paris and the Helen Drutt Collection.
Since 1998, Florence's jewellery has considered the theme of birth, and her work revolves around the analogy between the birth of forms and the birth of human beings, between creation and procreation.

Carole Leonard
British
caroleleonardjewellery@gmail.com
www.caroleleonardjewellery.co.uk

Carole graduated from Hornsey College of Art (now Middlesex University) with a degree in Three-dimensional Design (Silversmithing) and has been earning her living as a jeweller ever since.
Her work shows the influence of the silversmith's aesthetic. Ideas develop from the process of making and the properties and potential of the materials used – perspex, silver, steel and gold. Carole is particularly interested in the affect of body chemistry and daily circumstance on different surfaces and how each piece of jewellery matures with wear. She has combined precious and non-precious materials in her work to exploit this process. Recent Arts Council funding has given her the opportunity to reassess her work and research the use of steel in contemporary jewellery.

Anna Lewis
British
info@annalewisjewellery.co.uk
www.annalewisjewellery.co.uk

Anna Lewis graduated from Middlesex University in 2000 and has become well known for her delicate printed feather, leather and wood creations.

She has exhibited throughout the UK in some of the best contemporary craft galleries and at events such as Chelsea Crafts Fair. She has also exhibited internationally in France, the USA, Kuwait, Germany, Japan, Milan and Australia. Anna's jewellery has been featured in several magazines including *Elle Decoration, Living Etc. Wedding & Home, You, Embroidery, Selvedge* and *Crafts.*

Memory, memorial, amulets and shrines are interconnecting themes that inspire Anna's work. She is interested in the relationship people have with certain objects and how they influence belief through their material meanings.

Tina Lilienthal
German
info@tinalilienthal.com
www.tinalilienthal.com

Since graduating from the Royal College of Art in 2003 Tina Lilienthal has shown her work at a variety of contemporary jewellery exhibitions in the UK and abroad, and her collections are featured in galleries in the UK, Europe, Canada and Japan. She has lectured at the Royal College of Art and Coventry University, and is currently a senior lecturer at London Metropolitan University. Her work has been awarded the Marzee Prize, 2003; the first prize for Fashion Jewellery in the Goldsmiths' Craftsmanship and Design Awards, 2004; and the first Prize in the Holts Jewellery and Design Awards, 2005.

Through the unconventional mixture of materials, Tina's work tells the story of the cheap and the expensive, the old and the new, the mundane and the precious, the sacred and the profane. Despite the highly wearable nature of her work an element of humour and playfulness

clearly shines through.

The end of 2007 sees Tina opening Studio North, a gallery space for contemporary, bespoke and conceptual jewellery, in collaboration with three other RCA graduates.

Micki Lippe
American
mickilippe@comcast.net
www.looselyhinged.com

For many years Micki has run a production studio shipping jewellery all over the US. Her work has been shown in numerous books and exhibitions. She has served as a board member of several jewellery related non-profit organizations, taught workshops and mentored young jewellers who began their careers working for her company, Loosely Hinged.

In the past few years she has also made one-of-a-kind jewellery. While living in the northwest of America Micki has been inspired by the random quality of nature, and moss, leaves, twigs, flowers and seedpods influence her work, which is also a reflection of her deep conviction in the importance of caring for our environment.

Alison Macleod
British
alison@alisonmacleod.com
www.alisonmacleod.com

Alison graduated from Edinburgh College of Art in 2003 with a First Class Honours degree. Now working from her studio in Glasgow, she exhibits in the UK and internationally.

Alison has a fascination with junk shops and flea markets. Each object she finds is a mysterious fragment of someone's past, its narrative enclosed

within the dents and scratches. It is these precious traces of the past that she aims to incorporate into her jewellery. Through using a wide range of materials, techniques and imagery, Alison reflects the eclectic nature of her subject matter in a quirky way.

Patricia Madeja
American
callahanmadeja@earthlink.net
www.patriciamadeja.com

Patricia Madeja received her BFA in 1985 from the Pratt Institute in New York and established her studio in 1989 on Long Island, where she designs and produces limited-edition collections in sterling, 14ct and 18ct gold. Her design inspiration derives from geometric forms and architectural structures, with movement as an integral component of each piece.

Patricia is the recipient of an MJSA Vision Award, AJDC Award, Saul Bell Award, Jewelry Arts Award and Niche Award and has been featured in a variety of periodicals and books including *500 Necklaces, Art Jewelry Today* and *The Art and Craft of Making Jewelry*. A strong advocate for jewellery education, she was invited by the Pratt Institute in 1998 to join the fine arts department as an adjunct professor and was recently appointed coordinator for the jewellery area.

Lindsey Mann
British
lindsey@lindseymann.co.uk
www.lindseymann.co.uk

Lindsey graduated from Middlesex University in 2002 with a First Class Honours degree in Jewellery. Since setting up her studio in 2003 she has exhibited throughout the UK and abroad and her work is featured in both public and private collections.

Lindsey's jewellery is made from anodized aluminium combined with silver and materials both found and formed. She employs traditional jewellery making techniques alongside modern digital printing processes that she has developed specifically for her work.

Amanda Mansell
Britain
amanda@amanda-mansell.com
info@dualpod.co.uk
www.amanda-mansell.com
www.dualpod.co.uk

Amanda Mansell graduated from the Royal College of Art in 1997, and has designed catwalk jewellery for fashion designers Julien McDonald and David Fielden. She has received publicity in magazines such as *Marie Claire*, *Cosmopolitan*, *Elle* and American *Vogue*, and features in the *Design Sourcebook: Jewellery*, by David Watkins and *Art and Design: 100 Years of the Royal College of Art* by Sir Christopher Frayling.

Amanda operates her jewellery design business from her studio in Hatton Garden, London. In May 2005 she opened DualPod, a contemporary jewellery gallery in Islington, London, where she sells her own and other designers' work. Her work subtly combines precious and non-precious materials in a minimal, geometric and graphic format, inspired by architectural and natural forms.

Hayley Mardon
British
hayleymardon@hotmail.com
www.hayleymardon.com

Hayley graduated in 2007 with a First Class Honours from Edinburgh College of Art, where she also won a Precious Metal Bursary Award from the Goldsmiths' company. She is the senior in-house designer at Made, a fair-trade jewellery company, and works in London and with artisans in Nairobi. Her designs for Made have been featured in magazines such as *Marie Claire*, *Grazia* and *Telegraph Magazine* and are currently on sale in Topshop. Hayley was recently awarded winner of the ACJ Associate Prize at New Designers 2007, and was selected to take part in the Standard Life 'BraveArt' exhibition at the Atlantis Gallery, London, 2007.

Hayley's work is colourful, bold and painterly, and is inspired by her childhood memories of growing up in Zimbabwe.

Susan May
British
susan@susanmay.org
www.susanmay.org

Susan May studied jewellery at Middlesex University in the late 1970s and spent a further year apprenticed to a Hatton Garden jewellery company, before setting up her own London studio.

Over the years Susan's work has evolved as a result of her many technical experiments with various metals, including blacksmithing. The methods she now uses allow her to capture the energy she sees in natural forms.

Judy McCaig
British
judmccaig@yahoo.com

Judy studied at Duncan of Jordanstone College of Art and Design, Dundee, and graduated in 1980. After completing a postgraduate year she studied at the Royal College of Art from 1980 to 1983. She established her own workshop in London at 401½ Workshops. She exhibits her work internationally and has participated in various European and American symposia.

In 1991 Judy moved her workshop to Barcelona where she now lives. She teaches regularly at the Massana School in Barcelona and at Edinburgh College of Art. Her work is in a number of collections and she exhibits in solo and group exhibitions.

Rowan Mersh
British
info@rowanmersh.com
www.rowanmersh.com

Rowan Mersh is a textile-based sculptor who explores form and fuses design with technique, emphasizing experimentation as the focus of his practice. Mersh is a celebrated graduate of the Royal College of Art (2005), the first to win the Mercury Art Prize and profiled in numerous design magazines and publications.

Mersh's work is process oriented, the work reveals itself within his practice, as it takes form and shape depending on the emphasis and materials.

258

Isabelle Metaxa
Greek/Australian
isabellametaxa@hotmail.com
www.myspace.com/foreignfeatures

Isabelle Metaxa graduated from the Birmingham Institute of Art and Design in 1999 and was later accepted as an Artist in Residence at the London Metropolitan University. Between 2003 and 2005 Isabelle formed a workshop in Athens, Greece, and participated in the annual international Schmuck exhibition for contemporary jewellery in Munich in 2005. Her work has featured in the books *500 Necklaces*, published by Lark Books and *Art Jewellery Today*, from Schiffer Publishing.

Isabelle concentrates on one-off pieces and collections, each time applying a new medium accordingly while developing the overall style.

Bruce Metcalf
American
bruce_metcalf@verizon.net

Bruce Metcalf makes jewellery using simple shapes and surfaces painted with blatantly decorative patterns. The idea is to produce jewellery that is equally beautiful and strange. Metcalf uses images of fruits, leaves, buds and bodies in his work to suggest fecundity, with an overtone of sexuality. In addition, the comparatively large size of this jewellery is highly theatrical, placing wearers and watchers in a drama of their own invention.

Louise Miller
British
info@louisemiller.co.uk
www.louisemiller.co.uk

Louise Miller graduated from the Royal College of Art in 2005. Louise produces pieces for exhibitions and galleries, developing ways in which two-dimensional surface decoration can be translated into contemporary jewellery. She is often drawn to non-precious materials such as plastic and paper, because they suit her methods of working and allow her to experiment with a wide spectrum of colours.

Helga Mogensen
Icelandic
helga_mogensen@hotmail.com
www.helgamogensen.com

Helga graduated from Edinburgh College of Art in 2007 with a First Class Honours degree in Jewellery and Silversmithing. Since graduating she has participated in numerous exhibitions and undertaken private commissions.

By using a range of different combinations of materials, Helga aims to create jewellery that reflects a personal interest in exploring colour combinations and compositions that challenge the viewer and wearer. Helga's work reflects a strong relationship with her family and a special hideaway place in the countryside of Iceland where she goes every summer.

Marc Monzó
Spanish
marcmonzo@hotmail.com
www.marcmonzo.net

Marc Monzó studied jewellery at the Massana School in Barcelona. Since his graduation in 1997 he has been working as an independent jewellery designer.

Marc has been professor of a workshop entitled 'The Big Bang and You' in the Konstfact Academie in Stockholm and has given lectures in several schools such as Hiko Mizuno College in Tokyo, the Gerrit Rietveld Academy in Amsterdam and the Antwerp Royal Academy.

Sonia Morel
Swiss
sonia.morel@hotmail.com

Sonia Morel, a graduate of the Applied Art School in Geneva, shuns the inflexible, immovable and definitive. She has an affinity with the 'crude' and fantastic in art. Her pieces are futuristic and historical at the same time sometimes taking inspiration from the hairstyles of the Egyptians or armor and helmets of Samourai warriors. The innumerable associations of her pieces are not the only fascinations for the spectator. Her pieces have playful movement and and a requirement for Sonia is that her pieces respect and adapt themselves to the body.

Jill Newbrook
British
jill@newbrook.co.uk

Jill Newbrook originally trained and worked as a graphic designer. She took a course in Art and

Design, specializing in jewellery, at the Sir John Cass School of Art, London, graduating in 1989. Since then she has worked from a shared workshop in north London.

Through her work Jill emphasizes surface decoration, while the shapes are kept simple and bold. Ancient Japanese textile prints are the inspiration for the photo-etched designs that are combined with textured gold. Usually the piece will evolve during the making process, and this can lead to further ideas and variations.

Evert Nijland
Dutch
evert.nijland@gmail.com

Evert Nijland graduated from the jewellery department at the Gerrit Rietveld Academy in Amsterdam in 1995 and continued his studies to Masters level at the Sandberg Institute in the city. His jewellery takes inspiration from images from art history, in particular the Renaissance and Baroque periods. He translates these images into his own contemporary context. He is fascinated by the way nature is visualized by artists, as illustrated in his 2006 work 'Venezia', which is based on his impressions of the city itself as well as its traditions in the field of visual art, design and architecture.

Helen Noakes
New Zealander
helennoakes@mac.com
www.helennoakesjewellery.com

A series of evening workshops, a part-time course and an award – Best Use of Metalwork and Techniques at the Victoria and Albert Museum's 'Inspired by...' competition, 1999 – lured jewellery designer/maker Helen Noakes from corporate London to a Wiltshire jewellery workbench in late 2004.

Since then her work has developed and evolved into complete collections of trademark quirky pieces – contemporary jewellery spiked with humour and tiny surprises. Helen uses miniature models as the nucleus of her designs, cast in resin or precious metals and set in simple, finely handcrafted silver settings. The hard-to-find figures that have become the focus of her collection run the gamut from penguins, scuba divers and terriers to cheeky punk rockers and 1900s' bathers. In 2006, Helen won the Best Jeweller Award at the acclaimed Bovey Tracey Contemporary Craft Fair.

Eun-Joo Noh
Korean
nonjoo97@hanmail.net

Eun-Joo graduated from Konkuk University and Kookmin Graduate University, majoring in Metal Crafts. Eun-Joo's jewellery has featured in many group and solo exhibitions in Seoul, and she has received awards at the Ssamziegil Design Contest, Korea, 2004, and ITAMI International Craft Exhibition, Japan, 2002. She currently works as a jewellery designer at the Leeum Samsung Museum of Art, and owns her own brand, Early Bird.

Eun-Joo creates jewellery as a medium for communication between her and the wearer. Her work often features a variety of joining devices related to the 'wearing' of jewellery, spatial structures that are then developed, overlapped or hidden like a puzzle.

Simone Nolden
German
simone_nolden@hotmail.com
www.simonenolden.com

Simone trained as a gold- and silversmith in Cologne prior to taking a degree in Jewellery and Product Design at the University of Applied Arts in Dusseldorf. In 2005 Simone received a Crafts Council Development Award and has set up a studio in Sheffield, where she designs and makes jewellery for exhibition and sale.

Discovering things in unlikely settings is the main inspiration behind her work. She enjoys exploring the past history of everyday objects. Her work merges the non-precious and precious: iron nails and old keys may be juxtaposed with a range of precious materials and gems to create jewellery that challenges the traditional concept of value.

Ted Noten
Dutch
info@tednoten.com
www.tednoten.com

Ted Noten is a jewellery designer who constantly explores the boundaries of his profession. Once a bricklayer and a psychiatric nurse, he graduated from the Amsterdam Gerrit Rietveld Academy in 1990. Noten has participated in a number of exhibitions in the Netherlands and abroad, and his work is included in several private and public collections.

Sawing up a Mercedes Benz car to make brooches and sealing a dead mouse wearing a tiny pearl necklace inside a block of acrylate, Ted's work courts controversy. Still, Noten honours the specific qualities of jewellery design, in which emotions and small stories play the leading part.

Contributors

Carla Nuis
Dutch
carla@carlanuis.nl
www.carlanuis.nl

Educated as a professional goldsmith and an artist at the Maastricht Academy of Art (BA, 1995) and the Royal College of Art (M.Phil., 2005), Carla Nuis now operates her own workshop in Haarlem, the Netherlands. Her work is exhibited in internationally renowned galleries, including Marzee, Charon Kransen, Electrum and Deux Poissons, and widely published in professional books and magazines. It has been acquired by private collectors and for public collections, including the Victoria and Albert Museum. Carla Nuis received the 2005 Nicole Stöber Memorial Award and the Dutch Design Award 2006 for Jewellery and Fashion.

In her recent work, 'Objectification of Ornamentation', Nuis seeks to enhance the grandeur of classic two-dimensional ornamental textile patterns through their transformation into open worked, three-dimensional precious metal jewellery objects.

Kati Nulpponen
Finnish
katinulpponen@gmail.com
www.amazinganimal.fi

Kati graduated as a jeweller in Lappeenranta, Finland in 1996. Together with two other jewellers, she is a member of the artists' group Amazing Animal, and has participated in numerous exhibitions since 2002. Most recently she has represented her country in the Ars Ornata Europeana exhibition 2007.

Kati's work comes close to contemporary visual art without losing its character as jewellery. Using materials such as porcelain, crochet and duck webs, it reminds us of the fragile strength of the mortal body. Within her works she also explores the differences between femininity and masculinity, innocence and violence, and me and you.

Sean O'Connell
Australian
sean@oneorangedot.com
www.oneorangedot.com

Sean is an Australian jeweller whose work concerns itself broadly with restriction and freedom, and in a more basic sense, order and chaos. The generative concepts of the works may take a specific focus, such as current work dealing with the skeletons of radiolarians, or a more general approach, such as past work concerned with creating a tactile sense of dense fluidity in jewellery. The actual making of his work is a core component in its generation, the materials and processes dancing with the ideas and concepts brought to the workbench.

Meghan O'Rourke
Australian
meghanorourke@iprimus.com.au
www.myspace.com/meghanorourkejewellery

Meghan is an associate designer with the prominent JamFactory Metal Design Studio in Adelaide, Australia, and has gained recognition with various fine art awards and international residencies.

As a contemporary jeweller and metalsmith, Meghan O'Rourke aims to create precious objects for the body that are both playful and ornate. Her refined and colourful jewellery explores the use of patterns derived from the delicate structures found in nature, primarily plants and coral. Meghan's work often combines the fascinating optical effects and vivid colour palette of anodized titanium and aluminium with more traditional materials. Additionally, the hand dying and subtle texturing techniques that she has developed give the process a sense of spontaneity, ensuring that no two pieces are ever exactly the same.

Emiko Oye
Japanese/Euro American
rewarestyle@mac.com
www.rewarestyle.com

Inspired by hardware, haute couture, and salvaged materials, Emiko Oye creates one-of-a-kind urban jewellery and conceptual sculptures from recycled materials and precious metals. Her works strive to subtly transform the identity of everyday mundane objects to create new dialogues about our relationship with the environment. Oye's jewellery features in Lark Book's *Fabulous Jewelry from Found Objects* and *The Art of Jewelry: Plastic and Resin*, as well as in *Metalsmith* magazine, *The Crafts Report*, and *American Craft*.

Hiroko Ozeki
Japanese
ozekihiroko@hotmail.com

Hiroko Ozeki graduated from the Royal College of Art in 2001 and works and lives in London. Her work is featured in galleries in the UK and Europe.

Through research and experimentation with unexpected materials, Hiroko seeks to express unique visual and physical characteristics. In her work with iron wire she has developed her own fabrication and finishing techniques that enable the material to become lace-like, delicate and complex, transcending our expectations.

Barbara Paganin
Italian
paganinb@hotmail.com

Barbara graduated from the Academy of Fine Arts in Venice and now teaches jewellery design at the Venice School of Art. Her works have appeared in a selection of books and she has participated in a number of exhibitions including Jewellery Moves, Edinburgh; Schmuck, Munich, 1999 and 2003; and SOFA, New York and Chicago. Her works also feature in a number of collections, including Boymans Van Beuningen in Rotterdam, Musée des Arts Décoratifs in Paris, the Montreal Decorative Arts Museum, Schmuckmuseum Pforzheim and Cooper-Hewitt National Design Museum in New York.

Barbara's jewellery is inspired by nature with geometrical structure and infused with her own emotions and experiences.

Jieun Park
Korean
jieun624@hanmail.net

Jieun graduated from Konkuk University in 2004 and went on to study at the graduate school there. Since then she has participated in a number of exhibitions and continued to develop her personal style.

Jieun's jewellery considers questions of social phenomena and studies the image of human beings and how it changes with different societies.

Inni Pärnänen
Finnish
info@inni.fi
www.inni.fi

Inni Pärnänen graduated from the University of Industrial Arts in Helsinki in 1998 with a Masters degree and now actively participates in exhibitions in Finland and abroad. In 2005 she was awarded in the Unique Design competition for young jewellers, arranged by the Finnish Jewellers' Association.

Inni's work has aroused interest with her innovative and skilled use of materials, such as parchment and cow's horn. For her, the most important aspects in jewellery design are structure and functionality, which largely define how each jewellery piece is worn.

Betty Pepper
British
bettypepper@hotmail.com

Betty graduated from the University of Central England in Birmingham with a First Class Honours degree in Silversmithing and Jewellery Design. After winning the Gesellschaft Fuer Goldschmiedekunst Youth Promotion first prize in 2004 she set up her studio in Ipswich, where she now designs and makes her own jewellery. Betty exhibits both nationally and internationally and also works to commission. She has featured in magazines such as *Elle Decoration* and *Crafts*.

Betty describes her work as a hybrid that links textiles, fine art and jewellery and combines traditional jewellery skills with textile techniques. She uses word games, hidden messages and secrets to weave layers of memories and nostalgia through her pieces, and is inspired by the notion

that all things are constantly in a state of deterioration.

Felicity Peters
Australian
felicity@felicitypeters.com
www.felicitypeters.com

Felicity graduated from Curtin University of Technology in Western Australia in 1986. Her jewellery has featured in numerous books and she is represented in international and Australian public collections. Felicity has won many Australian awards, and received professional development grants from the Australia Council, the Government of Australia's arts funding body and ArtsWA, the arts funding body of the West Australian government.

Felicity's signature is her use of keum boo 24ct gold sheet fused to sterling silver, and her work is often humorous, making a statement about social and political issues.

Lina Peterson
Swedish
mail@linapeterson.com
www.linapeterson.com

Since leaving the Royal College of Art in 2006 Lina has exhibited her jewellery in Britain, the United States, Europe and Japan.

The main focus of Lina's work lies within the exploration of material qualities and combinations. One of the outcomes of her investigations is the 'Dipped' series, where sheet-metal and wire structures are covered with a brightly coloured plastic coating, creating playful and intriguing pieces of jewellery.

Natalya Sergeevna Pinchuk
Russian
npinchuk@yahoo.com
npinchuk@vcu.edu

Natalya graduated from the University of Illinois at Urbana-Champaign in 2005 and has since then exhibited her work with Charon Kransen Arts at SOFA, Chicago and New York; Galerie Rob Koudijs, Amsterdam; and Jewelers'Werk, Washington DC. Her work featured on the cover of the 2004 Exhibition in Print issue of *Metalsmith* magazine. Currently Natalya teaches at Virginia Commonwealth University, USA.

In her jewellery Natalya attempts to balance attraction and repulsion, beauty and criticism, laughter and sarcasm. In the 'Growth' series she combines wool, plastic and enamelled copper forms into miniature landscape systems. The wearing of these simulated 'growths' creates an ironic act of assimilation: the artificial becomes absorbed into the landscape of one's body.

Annelies Planteijdt
Dutch
anneliesp@zeelandnet.n

Annelies graduated from the Vakschool Schoonhoven in the Netherlands in 1977 and from the Gerrit Rietveld Academy in Amsterdam in 1983. She has been exhibiting her work since 1982. Annelies is fascinated by the fact that everything has an inner structure, even though it may not be obvious from the outside. She likes to look for structures and laws, and then make her own arrangements. The map that she thinks up for a piece of jewellery may seem to disappear when the jewellery is worn, but the structure remains.

Jo Pond
British
jo@jopond.com
www.jopond.com

Jo Pond graduated from the Birmingham School of Jewellery in 2005 with an MA Distinction in Jewellery, Silversmithing and Related Products. As well as continuing her professional practice as a designer/maker, Jo is a part-time university lecturer. Jo won the 2005 BDI Industry & Genius Awards in the category of Products and Genius. Jo is interested in the ambivalent perceptions of beauty. Utilizing a collection of unconventional objects and an aesthetic inspiration drawn from the unintended details of decomposition and change, she chooses to incorporate inconsistent, unambiguous items, to create beautiful yet disconcerting objects, focusing on the vulnerability of imperfection. By incorporating natural materials, Jo considers the state of impermanence, allowing nature and time to influence her design process.

David Poston
British
david.poston@iname.com

David Poston trained as a jewellery designer at Hornsey College of Art in London from 1967 (initially under Gerda Flöckinger) and worked as a non-precious, applied-art jeweller from 1972 until 1984. Deviating in order to contribute to the development of rural manufacturing and sustainable livelihoods in Africa, David made almost no further jewellery until 2000, when he began a three-year stint as the leader of a university silversmithing and jewellery programme.

Although continuing to make professional short-term visits to Africa, since 2003 David has progressively explored the statement inherent in presenting jewellery 'as worked', increasingly abstaining from post-manufacturing refinement and the concealment of process. Some narrative elements are also now included in order to pose questions and provoke responses.

Ramon Puig Cuyàs
Spanish
puigcuyas@gmail.com
puigcuyas.blogspot.com

Ramon has been teaching at the school he originally graduated from, the Massana School in Barcelona, since 1977, and he is now head of the jewellery department. His jewellery has been shown in numerous solo and prestigious group exhibitions at an international level, and his works are part of many public and private collections.

Enigmatic and mysterious, his latest works, entitled 'Walled Gardens', depict a glimpse of what we are able to see of gardens through iron gates or over high walls. Each piece in this series evokes the microcosms of plants that grow enclosed within imaginary landscapes: a play on what is seen and unseen, what is real or fantasy.

Loukia Helena Richards
British/Greek
loukiarichards@yahoo.com
www.photostore.org.uk/seCVPG.aspx?MID=112833

Loukia Richards graduated from the Berlin School of Fine Arts in 1993, and initially worked in the media. In 2002 she decided to focus all her energy on painting and art jewellery. She has participated in various exhibitions including

Heirlooms, London, 2006; the Brighton Craft Fair, 2006; and Diana Porter Contemporary Jewellery, Bristol, 2006.
She has been awarded several grants and is a Crafts Council Photostore Selected Maker, 2006.

Loukia is inspired by the embroidery tradition of Greece, her mother's country of origin. Her jewellery is a game of inventing something precious in form and meaning from an unexpected material.

Jacqueline Ryan
British
jacqueline-ryan@libero.it
www. Jacqueline-ryan.com

Jacqueline Ryan graduated with an MA from the Royal College of Art in 1991. She has since gone on to build a successful jewellery business showing at numerous exhibitions around the world, and has also won a number of awards.

In her work she abstracts nature and seeks to communicate brief impressions of what she has observed and encountered. She continually collects visual information about nature's forms, structures, surfaces, textures and colours, and translates the elements that most inspire her into jewellery. Much of her work is made up of moveable, tactile elements that shake, rattle and vibrate as the body moves: it is the interaction of the wearer with the work that truly brings the piece to life and completes its function.

Mette Saabye
Danish
mette@saabye.biz
www.saabye.biz

Mette Saabye graduated from the Jewellery Institute in 1997 and since then has been working with jewellery as an artistic expression. About her latest work she says: 'Illusion is a reality, if you choose it to be. Reality is what we make it, each of us, every second. Jewellery functions as a projection of desire, wishes and dreams. Jewellery has become my language.'

Kayo Saito
Japanese
info@kayosaito.com
www.kayosaito.com

After graduating from Musashino Art University in 1992, Kayo Saito worked as a tableware designer in Tokyo. She moved to London to study contemporary jewellery and graduated from the Royal College of Art in 2001, where she researched paper jewellery and looked at other materials with the same integrity as paper but greater durability. Since then her works have been exhibited across Europe, the US and Japan, and featured in the book *New Directions in Jewellery* and a series of jewellery books from Lark Books.

Kayo's jewellery reflects what she sees in nature. She carefully chooses her materials to capture the forms, structure, movement, texture and sounds of the organic world, which are expressed as sculptural jewellery – jewellery that is complete on its own, as well as on the wearer's body.

Philip Sajet
Dutch
aa@auquai.com
www.auquai.com

Philip Sajet graduated from the Gerrit Rietveld Academy, Amsterdam, in 1981 and held his first solo show in 1986. His aim is to make classical contemporary and wearable jewellery: jewellery that is valid for all times and places yet clearly born in this time.

Margareth Sandström
Swedish
margarethsandstrom@hotmail.com
www.sandstrom-dewit.com

Margareth Sandström has the finely honed precision of a skilled and experienced jeweller. She uses a saw blade to create small patterns of rhythmic angles, spirals and lines and possesses a sovereign mastery of tiny movements. Her elliptical bubbles, vigorous buds and rounded discs are elements in veritable flow. Form grows out of form, is deconstructed, varied, twists and turns and suddenly becomes something quite different.

Lucy Sarneel
Dutch
l.sarneel@planet.nl

Lucy Sarneel studied at the Stadsacademy in Maastricht and graduated from the Gerrit Rietveld Academy in Amsterdam in 1989.

Lucy works predominantly with zinc, but also with textiles, wood and paint. The basic ideas for her jewellery derive from daily life experiences, and her jewellery has an object-like character that provides stories and symbols with a universal character. She is fascinated by artificiality of nature, which results in forms that remind us of flowers, plants or twigs.

Claude Schmitz
Luxembourger
claude.schmitz@pt.lu
www.claudeschmitz.com

Claude Schmitz graduated from Antwerp Royal Academy in 1999 and the Royal College of Art in 2001. Since then he has worked as an independent artist and designer in Luxembourg. He has shown his jewellery in both group and solo exhibitions in Europe, the USA and Japan.

The concept of his work revolves around the ideas of tradition, values, possession, status and a matter of scale and weight. He does not intend to tell a whole story – he provides the ingredients, the rest is a matter of interpretation. His clean, formal idiom often embraces the circle as a point of departure and return.

Frederike Schürenkämper
German
fschuerenkaemper@gmx.de
www.frederikeschürenkämper.de

Frederike Schürenkämper graduated from the Hochschule für Gestaltung Pforzheim in 2006 and has been exhibiting her jewellery and fine arts nationally and internationally since 1999.

Frederike uses traditional materials such as precious metals, enamel and stones, but in contrast to conventional goldsmithing, which is often well thought out, her work is more intuitive. Often the work pieces remain unfinished for an uncertain time until the next step reveals itself.

Sonja Christine Seidl
German
sonjaseidl@paradis.dk
www.sonjaseidl.com

Originating from a traditional background as a silversmith and craftsman, Sonja explored her ideas in an experimental way at the Royal College of Art from 2002 to 2004, and has now established a workshop to move her initial concepts forward. She has won several awards and her work has appeared in a number of publications.

Sonja chooses whatever technique, object or material suits her idea, but focuses on crafting in metal, where she sees many possibilities still open. Inspiration is taken from 'growing ornaments' and 'containers', such as seed cases in nature, or from fashion cutting patterns.

Katja Seitner
Austria
katja.seitner@seitner.co.at
www.seitner.co.at

Katja graduated from the Royal College of Art in 2001 and moved back to Austria to continue her work in the family business. She designs and produces jewellery in a wide range of materials, particularly stainless steel, and designs her own stonecuts. She has participated in a number of exhibitions, such as 'Turning Point' (curated by Fritz Maierhofer and Susanne Hammer), a solo exhibition at Galerie Orfèo in Luxembourg, and 'Austrian Jewellery' at the Electrum Gallery in London. In 2006 she opened her own jewellery shop in the centre of Vienna, where she designs new collections and undertakes private commissions.

Karin Seufert
German
kgseufert@gmx.de
www.karinseufert.de

Karin graduated from the Gerrit Rietveld Academy in Amsterdam in 1995 and worked in the city until 1998, when she moved back to Berlin. She has participated in a number of national and international exhibitions in galleries and museums.

In her jewellery the significance of a very specific material takes the foreground: a material whose previous use evokes a certain story. Often an alienation arises from a familiar material being given an unusual shape, or a familiar shape being made in an unusual material, or even by the simple combination of used and new material.

Sarah Stafford
British
sarah@sarahstafford.co.uk
www.sarahstafford.co.uk

Designer and maker Sarah Stafford is one of the UK's leading lights in the field of classic contemporary and bespoke jewellery. Since graduating from London Guildhall University Sarah has exhibited extensively in the UK, US, Europe and Japan. She maintains a studio in London and a workshop on the south coast of England, and teaches jewellery making to private clients.

Sarah fuses traditional skills and modern techniques to create striking and beautiful pieces, with a strong emphasis placed on the quality of workmanship and originality of design. Her collection assimilates classic Japanese iconography, such as cherry blossom and wave forms, bringing an engaging new lightness of touch to a design collection that remains quintessentially unique.

Lesley Strickland
British
lesley@lesley-strickland.co.uk
www.lesley-strickland.co.uk

Lesley is a British jeweller specializing in the use of cellulose acetate (derived from cotton oil) combined with sterling silver. Her passion for designing and making jewellery started in 1976 at The City Literary Institute, London. Since then she has continued to evolve and develop her personal style.

Lesley's inspiration predominantly comes from weathered, natural forms, although the sculptures of Barbara Hepworth, Alexander Calder, Constantin Brancusi and Isamu Noguchi, and the photographs of Karl Blossfeldt have influenced her latest work. The methods Lesley uses are traditional jewellery techniques coupled with industrial processes and ones of her own invention, such as hand thermo-forming.

Barbara Stutman
Canadian
bstutman@sympatico.ca

Barbara studied fine arts and art history at the Montreal Museum of Fine Arts, Saidye Bronfman Centre and Concordia University, and metalworking with a variety of teachers in Canada and the United States.

For the past 20 years she has been creating jewellery using textile techniques, such as crochet and knitting, to convey her interest in things societal, political or environmental. She designed

her 'Royal' series, inspired by the jewellery of the maharajas of India, to consist of imposing, visually rich pieces whose value does not depend on the presence of gold, platinum or actual gemstones.

Barbara's work has been published in numerous art journals, catalogues and books, and is in the collections of the Museum of Arts and Design in New York, the Montreal Museum of Fine Arts, the Koch Ring Collection in Switzerland and La Musée du Québec in Quebec City.

Nelli Tanner
Finnish
nelli.tanner@elisanet.fi

Nelli Tanner was educated in jewellery and stonework at South Carelia Polytechnic, in Lappeenranta in Finland. She continued her studies in jewellery at the Gerrit Rietveld Academy in Amsterdam and graduated in 2003. She now works in Helsinki.

Tanner exhibits in Finland and abroad, and also undertakes installation work. Her jewellery is inspired by found objects, storytelling and spaces and distances between people.

Louise Seijen ten Hoorn
Dutch
louise@luzzious.com
www.luzzious.com

Louise set up her business designing and making jewellery in 2006, and since then the Goldsmiths' Craft and Design Council have awarded her for her sculptural arm pieces two years in a row.

Louise's 'art for the arm' is made by manipulating silver shapes into curvy, bold, wearable statement pieces. Her new work features a sleek, elegant silver bangle, with an

interchangeable acrylic colour element, which can be changed according to mood or outfit. Louise draws inspiration from geometry and modernism. A shape or idea comes to mind and evolves through the making of paper models until finalized in metal.

Salima Thakker
Belgian
salima.thakker@skynet.be
www.salimathakker.com

A graduate of the Royal Academy of Fine Arts, Antwerp, and the Royal College of Art, Salima Thakker exhibits her jewellery at galleries and fairs across the world. Salima teaches at the Academy of Fine Arts in the goldsmithing and metalwork department, and has designed collections for jewellery and watch brands. Her jewellery has won industry awards and receives regular coverage internationally in books and magazines.

The fine and delicate craftsmanship of Salima's work is reflected in the beauty and diversity of her creations. Where some pieces are tactile and rough, others are dynamic, soft and more approachable.

Rachelle Thiewes
American
rthiewes@elp.rr.com

Rachelle Thiewes' jewellery is in the permanent collections of several museums, including the Smithsonian American Art Museum and National Museums of Scotland, and can be found in numerous publications, including *Design Sourcebook: Jewellery* by David Watkins, *Jewellery Moves* by Amanda Game and Elizabeth Goring and *Jewelry in Europe and America* by Ralph

266

Turner. She has been a professor at the University of Texas at El Paso since 1976.

Rachelle's 'Mirage' series is based on the interplay of light and shadow and the resulting distortions of reality. A bracelet form has been made and photographed at different times of the day and year, capturing its shadow in its many different forms as the sun tracks across the sky. These shadows are then transformed into linear brooches, which refer to their dimensional origin.

Terhi Tolvanen
Finnish
terhitolvanen@gmail.com
www.terhitolvanen.com

Terhi graduated with an MA from the Sandberg Institute in Amsterdam in 1999.

Terhi's work is inspired by her love of the beauty in nature and represents the interaction between man and nature, focusing not on the damage caused by man but on care and preservation. She combines silver and gold with an amazing array of unusual materials, and treats them all in an unconventional and playful way, but always with great weight on details.

Ruth Tomlinson
British
ruth@ruthtomlinson.com
www.ruthtomlinson.com

During Ruth's studies at the Royal College of Art she developed her 'Encrustations' series, inspired by stories of shipwrecks and forgotten underwater worlds. Ruth uses jewels and colours of the sea – pearl, coral and aquas – combined with silver to create a collection that conveys the transient cycle of nature, growth, life and decay.

Karola Torkos
German
info@karakola.com
www.karakola.com

Karola graduated from the Royal College of Art in 2006 and her jewellery has been honoured with several awards, such as the Conran Foundation Award. Karola exhibits internationally and her work is in public and private collections.

The idea of variable jewellery is the focus of Karola's collection. To change the appearance of jewellery offers a facet of interaction or play between wearer and jewellery, and reaches beyond simple display on the body. The wearer decides on the look of the piece: a certain mood or preference for a colour or pattern can be an impetus.

Fabrizio Tridenti
Italian
fabriziotridenti@alice.it
www.klimt02.net/jewellers/index.php?item_id=8307

In 1982 Fabrizio graduated from the Istituto Statale d'Arte of Penne, Italy, with a degree in Jewellery Design. He then won a scholarship from Nicola da Guardiagrele Award, and after many years of apprenticeship with various goldsmiths opened his own contemporary jewellery workshop. He has exhibited internationally and his works feature in various publications, including the book *The Art of Jewellery: Wood* by Terry Taylor, and magazines.

Fabrizio's work is the result of a constant search for new techniques, new materials and new forms. He uses recycled materials, ready-made and objet trouvé, loves strong contrasts, extreme architectures and impossible combinations.

Catherine Truman
Australian
ctsl@senet.com.au
www.charonkransenarts.com

Catherine Truman is co-founder of Gray Street Workshop in Adelaide, one of Australia's most significant contemporary jewellery studios. In 1990 Truman was awarded the Japan/South Australia Cultural Exchange scholarship and studied with contemporary netsuke carvers in Tokyo, while more recently she was awarded an Australia Council for the Arts Fellowship. She has exhibited widely nationally and internationally and is represented in a number of major national and international collections.

Truman's work centres on the study of human movement and the history of anatomical representation and the resulting jewellery, carved from wood or wax evoke sensory responses of physical recognition and resemblance.

Liz Tyler
British
liztyler@mac.com
www.liztyler.com

Harmonious balance and continuity of line are the essential design elements of Liz Tyler's jewellery. Liz established her business in 1989 specializing in the anticlastic raising techniques that she had learned under Michael Good in Maine, USA. Two curves are hammered up in opposite direction in fine gauge metal, creating a strong yet flexible form. Liz combines these with forged and cast sections, sometimes incorporating gemstones which may be pre-set and lasered into position. Well known for her distinctive ring sets, Liz likes the metal to wrap around the finger and rise to become the setting for the stone, so there is no interruption in the flow of the design. Liz has won several awards including Best Design in Diamonds and Designer of the Year at the UK Jewellery Awards, and her work has appeared in many exhibitions and collections featuring the finest of British design.

Carolina Vallejo
Danish
mail@carolinavallejo.dk
www.carolinavallejo.dk

Carolina Vallejo is co-owner of Aurum, a gallery and workshop of contemporary jewellery in Copenhagen. She has received numerous prizes for her work, which has been shown in most of Europe, Cuba and Japan. She also guest teaches and gives lectures internationally.

   Carolina makes jewellery and objects with references to art, philosophy and the current political agenda. She experiments with materials, the shapes and texture of the jewellery, and its symbolic value, considering major themes that deal with moral and ethical questions.

Jacomijn van der Donk
Dutch
info@jacomijnvanderdonk.nl
www.jacomijnvanderdonk.nl

Jacomijn graduated in 1991 from the Gerrit Rietveld Academy in Amsterdam and since then her work has been exhibited around the world and documented in numerous publications. The work of Jacomijn van der Donk has always had a strong relationship with nature, sharing an organic and sensual vividness. For her newest collection she uses nature as a direct source.

During forest walks she gathers small branches and, back in her atelier, transforms them so they become indistinguishable from real coral or bone. From this 'new' material flexible jewellery develops.

Felieke van der Leest
Dutch
www.feliekevanderleest.com

Felieke van der Leest is a trained metalsmith and graduated from the jewellery department at the Academy of Fine Arts in Amsterdam in 1996. She makes colourful and humorous jewellery and small objects. Her work has been highly regarded on the international jewellery scene for many years and is in museum and private collections around the world.

   Felieke combines plastic toy animals and metalsmithing techniques with her childhood love of crochet and needlework. She draws her inspiration from everyday events, filtered through a surreal sense of humour.

Machteld van Joolingen
Dutch
machteldvanjoolingen@xs4all.nl
www.machteldvanjoolingen.nl

Machteld studied jewellery at the Gerrit Rietveld Academy in Amsterdam and graduated with Honours in 1996.

   Her work deals with the underlying codes of jewellery. She combines imagery from the multicultural neighbourhood in which she works and lives with the visual bombardment of the media. The result is jewellery that refers to folklore and modern iconography. The materials and techniques are chosen to fit the design.

Machteld is one of the initiators of a jewellery group in Rotterdam that organizes projects and exhibitions with the emphasis on jewellery as a form of art, rather than a way of promoting the maker.

Truike Verdegaal
Dutch
mail@truikeverdegaal.com
www.truikeverdegaal.com

Truike Verdegaal graduated from the Gerrit Rietveld Academy in Amsterdam in 1992 after studying gold- and silversmithing and industrial design. Verdegaal's work now features in several public and private collections and appears in various books and magazines. She lectures at the Rietveld Academy and is a guest teacher at the Estonian Academy of Arts in Tallinn.

   Truike likes to combine, use and misuse forms, styles and materials until something new is born and often uses old items of jewellery to create contemporary pieces.

Babette von Dohnanyi
German
info@bd-jewellery.com
www.bd-jewellery.com

Babette studied gold- and silversmithing in Italy and Germany and opened her first studio in Florence. While designing and making her jewellery she continued her studies into new techniques, and her work has been featured in various magazines and books.
Babette works with silver, gold and gemstones and is inspired by architectual forms and conceptual minimal art.

Kathy Vones
German
info@kvones.com
www.kvones.com

After moving to Great Britain at the age of 16, Kathy graduated from the Edinburgh College of Art in 2006 with a First Class degree in Silversmithing and Jewellery. Since then she has exhibited her work nationally and internationally, including at the Goldsmiths' Fair 2007 in London. She is currently working as an Artist in Residence at the Edinburgh College of Art.

Kathy's fascination for the deep-sea environment was sparked by visiting the Tsukiji fish market in Tokyo. The colours, textures and patterns of the fragile jellyfish, insectoid spider crabs and giant octopi inspired her to develop a process with which to create brightly coloured silicone shapes embossed with surface patterns, which are combined with fragile wire structures. These shapes 'grow' into large jewellery sculptures on the body of the wearer.

Andrea Wagner
German
info@andreawagner.nl
www.andreawagner.nl

Since her graduation in 1997 from the Gerrit Rietveld Academy in Amsterdam, Andrea has opened her own studio in the city and participated regularly in international exhibitions.

Andrea likes to experiment with materials in order to create the intriguing appearance and surfaces necessary to communicate the stories or thoughts behind her work. This has led her to use pigmented and moulded resin, felt and textiles, a special amber and reconstructed amber, as well as bone china.

David Watkins
British
david.watkins@rca.ac.uk

David Watkins was educated as a sculptor and during the 1960s worked as a sculptor, a musician and in special effects for the film industry, as well as collaborating with Wendy Ramshaw to design and manufacture fashion jewellery.

Since the beginning of the 1970s his creative concentration has been on studio jewellery. His jewellery, which is noted for its combination of hand and advanced technological methods in a wide range of materials, can be found in numerous public collections around the world.

Between 1984 and 2006 David Watkins was Professor and Head of Department of Goldsmithing, Silversmithing, Metalwork and Jewellery at the Royal College of Art. He is now the college's Research Professor of Jewellery.

Günter Wermekes
German
info@wermekes.de
www.wermekes.de

From 1975 to 1978 Günter Wermekes trained as a goldsmith in the workshop of Professor Friedrich Becker, and later became his personal assistant and workshop head. In 1990 he set up his own workshop and began building up his jewellery collection. His work has won many prizes and pieces are featured in public and private collections.

Stacey Whale
New Zealander
stacey@staceywhale.com
www.staceywhale.com

Stacey studied at the School of Art and Craft Design in Wellington, New Zealand, graduating in 1999, and has lived and worked in London for the past eight years.

Stacey creates innovative male and female jewellery handcrafted in gold, which breathes an originality not seen in today's mass-produced and overly branded culture. The mysterious and the curious found in the natural and microscopic world provide a platform of inspiration for Stacey's jewellery. Among her signature pieces is Stacey's lens jewellery, which employs her award-winning original technique of sealing gems and other objects under a carefully polished lens, magnifying the precious contents encased within.

Francis Willemstijn
Dutch
info@willemstijn.com
www.willemstijn.com

Francis studied jewellery at the Gerrit Rietveld Academy in Amsterdam and graduated in 2004. Since then she has participated in a number of group and solo exhibitions, including Collect at the Victoria and Albert Museum and SOFA in New York and Chicago. Her work has been published in national and international books, catalogues and magazines.

Francis' work is based on Dutch history, although materials also play a big part, and wood is one of her favourites. As a reaction against mass-production she creates pieces that can not be reproduced, using unusual and often rare materials to produce her jewellery with an embedded memory and history.

Francis also creates websites for other jewellery artists and events.

Andrea Wippermann
German
a.wipp@web.de

From 1985 to 1991 Andrea Wippermann studied sculpture and three-dimensional design at the School for Art and Design Burg Giebichenstein in Halle, specializing in jewellery, and from 1992 to 1993 studied at postgraduate level in the same field. Since then she has taught the subject of jewellery in London and Switzerland.

Andrea Wippermann collects impressions that she brings to life in metal. Plants, animals, humans and architecture form central motifs in her creative oeuvre. Her works based on natural objects are characterized by lightness and fragility, while other pieces represent crumbling architectural structures.

Georgia Wiseman
British
georgia@georgiawiseman.com
www.georgiawiseman.com

Georgia Wiseman is an award-winning jewellery designer and maker who graduated from Glasgow School of Art in 2003 with a degree in Jewellery and Silversmithing.

Since establishing her workshop in Glasgow in 2005, assisted by the Scottish Arts Council and Prince's Trust, she has exhibited at Collect at the Victoria and Albert Museum and has recently been selected as a member of Design-Nation.
Georgia strives to encourage successful

relationships between the modern sharp lines of the metal structures she designs and the natural qualities of gemstones; geometric forms against the natural beauty of pearls.

Joe Wood
American
joewood@massart.edu
www.joewoodstudio.com

Joe Wood is currently the programme coordinator for the metals department at Massachusetts College of Art in Boston, and has taught jewellery, metalsmithing and computer techniques for object-makers there since 1985. He has hosted workshops in many prestigious art schools, including the Royal College of Art, Silpakorn University in Bangkok and Seattle Metals Guild, and exhibited at Schmuck 2001, Munich, and Signals: Late 20th Century American Jewelry at Cranbrook Museum of Art. His work is featured in public collections and has been widely published in catalogues, books and magazine articles. Joe Wood is represented by Mobilia Gallery, Cambridge, Massachusetts.

Lawrence Woodford
Canadian
muniya4@hotmail.com

Lawrence graduated with Honours from the École de Joaillerie et de Métaux d'Arts de Montréal in 1997, and that same year won Le Prix François Houdé as best emerging artist. He then taught at fine art institutions in Montreal until 2001, and now creates works for galleries in North America and abroad.

The trees, flowers and fruit found in nature, as well as tools, industrial design and even garbage

are Woodford's main inspiration. Drawing from these sources enables him to create the pieces he constructs and at times deconstructs. Often something that is discarded or viewed as worthless becomes the object of beauty.

Fiona Wright
British
fwright2003@yahoo.co.uk

Fiona graduated from London Metropolitan University in 2006 and now works with recycled newspaper in an innovative and experimental manner. Her work challenges the traditional perception of jewellery through using a non-precious material, and questions our perceptions of value through embracing contemporary ecological issues. Using only the colour of the print, the paper is spun by hand to form a yarn from which the pieces are then developed. Each piece contains a life cycle of stories: from wood to paper, the articles in newsprint, through the newspaper's journeys – purchased and read by one commuter, left on the train for another – to its transformation into a unique piece of contemporary jewellery. The final chapter is provided by the wearer, adding their personal expression of individuality.

Mizuko Yamada
Japanese
mizuko@grace.ocn.ne.jp

Mizuko studied traditional Japanese metalwork techniques and jewellery to degree level at Tokyo National University of Fine Arts and Music, before taking a Masters in silversmithing. He has been Artist in Residence at the Royal College of Art and Edinburgh College of Art.

Acknowledgements

Mizuko has had 20 years' experience as a jewellery artist and designer. He has designed, created and exhibited a variety of metal works for group or solo exhibitions, shows, and competitions both in Japan and internationally. These works include functional pieces and conceptual, avant-garde jewellery.

Mizuko also teaches metalwork, jewellery and design and established and administered the choukin decorative metalwork and jewellery programmes at Tama Art University in Japan.

Liaung-Chung Yen
Taiwanese
liaung@yahoo.com

Liaung-Chung Yen graduated from the Savannah College of Art and Design in 2001 and went on to work for jewellery artist Barbara Heinrich. He received a fellowship from the New York Foundation for the Arts in 2005, was a finalist in the NICHE Awards 2007 and took second place in the MJSA Vision Award in the Natural Colour Diamond Category in 2007. He features in the *Metalsmith* magazine 'Exhibition in Print' 2007, and the books *1000 Rings, 500 Brooches* and *500 Earrings*, published by Lark Books. He has participated in a number of exhibitions.

By using metaphor in his design, Liaung thinks of his jewellery as small expressions of art, desire, wit or sensuality. His current work explores the ability of line and pattern to create structure, form and motion.

Jung-gyu Yi
Korean
yijg195740@hanmail.net
www.heyri.net

From 1979 to 1984 Jung-gyu Yi studied jewellery design at the Fachhochschule Pforzheim in Germany. She majored in metal formative arts at the Ecole Nationale Supérieure des Arts Appliqués et des Métiers d'Art in Paris, from 1985 to 1989, and has since taught at several universities. Jung-gyu has participated in many exhibitions, including SOFA in Chicago and New York, and Schmuck, Munich. In 2006 she opened the jewellery gallery Baum and her studio in Heiry Art Valley, Korea.

Jung-gyu works with precious and non-precious materials, including diamonds, lapis lazuli, ivory, wood and whetstone.

Annamaria Zanella
Italian
zanella.annamaria@libero.it

Annamaria graduated from the Pietro Selvatico Institute of Fine Arts, Padua, in 1985 after studying jewellery, and in 1992 obtained the Diploma in Sculpture at the Academy of Arts in Venice. She won the Herbert Hofmann prize in Munich in 1997 and in 2006, and her highly expressive works of art are present in many of the most important museum collections in Europe and the USA.

The Italian Arte Povera movement inspires Annamaria's concept works, where precious and 'less precious' materials – silver, enamel, broken glass, resin, copper, gold, plastics, wood and paints – are transformed and modelled into provocative shapes and signs.

From beginning to end, there have been many who have helped me through this journey in numerous ways, from small words of encouragement over a glass of wine to invaluable expert advice, all of which helped get me through.

Sincere thanks must go to Beatriz Chadour for her valuable time and guidance, Jacqueline Scholes for her priceless assistance and notorious organisational skills, and Mum and Dad, as always, for their neverending support and words of encouragement. To all my friends, both personal and within the jewellery industry, for listening and being there during challenging periods, with heartfelt thanks to Laura Cave and Hannah Ball.

Thanks are also due to my commissioning editor at Laurence King Publishing, Helen Evans, for giving me the opportunity to undertake such an exciting project and to Peter Richardson for taking on board some of my early thoughts and professionally translating them into this wonderfully stylish design. And finally, underlying gratitude to the wonderfully talented artists around the world for their contributions and patience in helping put together this beautiful book. Thank you.

Picture Credits

images); 200 (left)
Laken, Birgit 24 (left); 25 (right)
Lamb, Hannah Louise 18 (left); 82 (bottom)
Lammas, Andrew 111 (top right)
Leane, Shaun 238
Lehmann, Florence 30 (left)
Leighton, Keith 13 (left and right); 19 (bottom left); 24 (bottom right); 41 (left); 44 (left); 49 (all images); 76 (both images); 102 (both images); 122 (top and bottom right); 142 (right); 184 (top right); 203 (top right and bottom left)
Low, Joe 62 (top left); 156 (bottom right); 213 (left)
Macove, James 145 (top left)
Mann, James 187 (top left)
Mansell, Amanda 40 (left); 124 (right); 177 (right); 198 (left)
©marzee 206 (right)
May, Susan 182 (left)
McGregor, John K. 29; 61 (top right); 103 (left); 119 (right)
McLean, Anthony 41 (right); 148 (top right)
Meara, Tim 195; 228 (left)
Meara, Tim (with many thanks to Jochen Braun and Joseph O'Brien) 17; 221
Merinero, Juan 56 (top left); 194 (right)
Metaxa, Isabelle 45 (top right)
Metcalf, Bruce 69 (both images); 130 (centre and right)
Mogensen, Helga 56 (top right); 91
Monzó, Marc 111 (bottom); 152 (both images)
Morton, Michael 207 (right)
Munch Studio 109 (all images); 123 (right)
Neuberger, Dan 216 (right)
Nielsen, Søren 42 (right); 83 (left); 183 (bottom left)
Nolden, Simone 181 (both images)
Noten, Atelier Ted 197 (right)
Nuis, Carla 121 (right)

O'Brien, Joseph see Meara, Tim (pp. 17, 221)
Paca, Albert 15 (right); 166; 197 (left)
Paca, Albert (credit collection of Charlotte Davy) 55
Paca, Albert (credit collection of Gene Sherman) 163
Pace, Lara 188 (left)
Park, Kwang-Choon 193 (both images)
Park, Kwangchun 113 (top left)
Pärnänen, Inni 75 (top left)
Pepper, Betty 68 (right)
Peterson, Lina 125 (all images)
PhotoIn Studio 135 (top left)
Pinchuk, Natalya 134 (bottom right); 135 (right)
Pond, Jo 99 (right)
Powell, Dean 153 (both images)
Rama 84; 85 (left); 86 (left)
Richards, Loukia 51 (centre); 81 (top left)
Riis, Rene 93 (right); 114 (bottom); 127 (right)
Rosa, Doug 226 (both images)
Rowe, Ben 15 (bottom left)
Rowe, Simon 14 (left); 117 (top right); 142 (left)
Rustichelli, Giulio 132 (right)
Ryan, Jacqueline 87 (left); 132 (left); 135 (bottom left)
Saito, Kayo 43 (left)
Sakwa, Hap 26 (left)
Sällberg, Jonas 52 (all images); 54 (left); 206 (left and centre)
Sällbers, Jonas 115 (top left); 122 (left); 200 (right); 201 (top left)
Schulze-Brinkop, Helga 45 (bottom); 57 (right); 75 (right); 87 (right); 129 (top left and right); 183 (top left); 189 (bottom)
Schwarz, Nicola 28 (right); 225; 227
Scrase, Andrew 19 (right); 46 (left and right)
Seaward, Jesse 92; 121 (left)
Seitner, Katja 154 (top left and bottom)
Seitsara, Jaan 59 (top left); 73 (right); 127 (left)
Seufert, Karin 51 (left); 74 (right); 108 (top right); 114 (top right); 116 (right)

Singleton, Edward 188 (right); 204 (right)
Stafford, Sarah 104 (right)
Storti, Franco 143 (bottom left)
Studio Monch 30 (right)
Sweeny, Dominic 202 (top left and bottom); 216 (left)
Tanner, Nelli 114 (top left)
Thakker, Salima 56 (bottom); 162 (top left and bottom); 191 (both images)
Thiewes, Rachelle 95 (right); 161 (all images)
Thurston, Frank 26 (right); 86 (right)
Tofts, Shannon 12 (left and right); 42 (left); 43 (right); 47 (left); 70 (both images); 165 (right); 215 (left)
Torkos, Karola 64 (right)
Tridenti, Fabrizio 22 (left); 124 (left); 147 (left); 189 (top left)
Tschudin, Dominic 33 (top left); 164 (left)
van Joolingen, Machteld 250 (both images)
Virardi, Filippo 39 (top); 78 (left)
Wagner, Andrea 128 (left); 136 (right)
Ward, Patrick 141; 194 (left); 198 (bottom right)
Watkins, David (CGI) 174; 175
Wenting, Eddy 66 (top left); 80 (centre)
Willemstijn, Francis 79 (top right and bottom); 94 (bottom right); 107 (top and bottom left); 147 (right)
Wills, Sarah 55 (right); 137 (bottom left); 156 (top left)
Wilson, Steve 32
Wilwert, Marc 23 (top right); 117 (bottom); 120 (right); 143 (top left and right); 190 (right)
Wiseman, Georgia 66 (bottom); 190 (left)
Wouters, Freija 239
Yen, Liaung Chung 25 (bottom left); 201 (bottom left)
Young, Kingmond 229
Zufferey, Thierry 77 (bottom); 82 (top left); 164 (right); 167 (right); 199 (top and bottom left)